WESTMAR COLLEGE LIBRARY

THE REFORM BILL OF 1832

THE REFORM BILL
OF 1832

Why Not Revolution?

Edited by WILLIAM HENRY MAEHL, JR.
The University of Oklahoma

HOLT, RINEHART AND WINSTON
New York · Chicago · San Francisco · Toronto · London

72796

328.42
M184

JN
218
.M3

Cover illustration: The Reform Bill of 1832 receiving the royal assent in the House of Lords. (*The Bettmann Archive*)

Copyright © 1967 by Holt, Rinehart and Winston, Inc.
All Rights Reserved
Library of Congress Catalog Card Number: 67–11301
25410–0117
Printed in the United States of America

72796

CONTENTS

The Handwriting on the Wall, May 26, 1831. One day
when William IV was taking his constitutional in the
park he came upon a sign painted on a wall. "Reform
Bill!" he exclaimed. "Could that mean me?" (*Cartoon
by J. Doyle; The Bettmann Archive*)

INTRODUCTION

On June 7, 1832, the Reform Bill of 1832 received the royal assent. Thus ended nearly two years of bitter controversy in Parliament and fierce agitation in every corner of the kingdom. Historians have long regarded passage of this bill as a major turning point in English history.

Since 1832 a tradition has grown up that England was on the brink of revolution during the reform struggle, and that revolution was averted only by a prudent concession of change by the old ruling oligarchy. Certainly many of the elements of revolution were present in England between 1830 and 1832 —a recent onslaught of economic distress, an aroused working class, a middle class disgruntled with the existing political system, an articulate and inflammatory Radical leadership, and a network of political unions designed to exert pressure for reform on the government. From time to time violence occurred and late in the course of passage of the Reform Bill through Parliament there were rumors of plans for an uprising if it was defeated.

Behind the immediate pressure for change lay more than half a century of frustration during which the quickening pace of industrialization rendered the representative system ever more anomalous and demands for reform were met with inexorable resistance on the part of the aristocracy. As early as the 1760s reformers had called for alteration of the representation in Parliament. Later they had been inspired by the revolution in France in 1789, only to have their hopes dampened by Pitt's wartime repression. Their cry rose again amid the postwar distress, but receded in the face of government controls and improving economic conditions during the 1820s. Then as the solidarity of the aristocracy declined at the end of the 1820s, the question revived and disturbed the tranquillity of the country until the bill's passage in 1832.

When reform agitation was resumed in 1830, the issue was not new, only the stridency with which it was urged. Midway through debate on the bill the inveterate memorialist Charles Greville recorded, "Hardinge, whom I found at dinner at the Athenaeum yesterday, told me he was convinced that a revolution in this country was inevitable; and such is the opinion of others who support this Bill, not because they think concession will avert it, but will let it come more gradually and with less violence." Half a century later

Justin McCarthy wrote, "It is hardly possible to doubt that during the reform struggle, England was brought once or twice very close to revolution." George Macaulay Trevelyan on the centenary of the Act commented, "Owing to the passage of the Bill, the cultivated upper class was not driven out of politics by violent revolution, as in America, France and elsewhere"; without it, he said, "Westminster would have been as the Tuileries."

If the revolutionary threat was that great, why did revolution not occur? Will the explanation of catastrophe forestalled by concessions of the aristocracy hold up? Were the very modest benefits granted the urban middle class enough to allay the popular fury that so many held in fear? Was the danger really genuine or was it an example of that hyperbole which people in the midst of great events sometimes allow themselves? What did men of various ranks expect from the reform of 1832? The passion aroused by debate in and out of Parliament has been matched by the strength of contrast in the interpretations of the episode and its significance. The selections that follow present some differing views on questions connected with the reform.

Historians are individualists and their works usually resist classification into clear-cut categories. In general, however, four major lines of interpretation can be seen in the writings on the Reform Bill period. The first, and perhaps most influential, is the Whig school, of which McCarthy and Trevelyan, quoted above, are good representatives. Coming to history from a Whig political tradition, they consider the reform as a triumph of moderation which preserved the best in English traditions and institutions while permitting necessary adaptation to change. They regard the changes of 1832 as the beginning of an evolution to modern democracy by peaceful means which avoided the class strife and disharmony that occurred in less fortunate countries. In the forefront of their accounts stands Parliament as the medium of change and accommodation.

Second, reflecting the opposition of the Tories to the Reform Bill, a group of writers of Tory sentiment question the undiluted optimism of the Whigs. While conceding the orderly adaptation of the Constitution after 1832, they nevertheless make a case for the good intentions of the Tory aristocrats who resisted change out of fear of unknown consequences. The Tories, they argue, knew better than the Whigs what the consequences of reform would be, and in its extreme form this view attributes stresses since 1832 to the Pandora's box that was opened by the Reform Act.

The third group are the historians of the working class. They see the reform in relation to the aspirations of the lowest stratum of English society and attribute its achievement largely to working-class efforts. Yet they stress that the working class did not benefit from the reform, and they see the Act only as a stage in the development of a working-class political movement.

In recent years the work of a fourth group has added new shadings to the reform controversy. More miscellaneous as a group than their predecessors, these historians can perhaps best be described collectively as revisionist, for they have singled out points in the traditional accounts for re-examination and fresh appraisal. Some of them have borrowed the methods of the social sciences. Others are simply good historians asking new questions concerning old evidence and probing beneath the surface of contemporary impressions. In some cases the revisionists differ sharply with one another, but they share one characteristic. They try to look at events in terms of their contemporary significance rather than from the perspective of hindsight, and their evaluations differ from traditional views based on political commitment.

The first group of selections gives four accounts of the reform struggle as a whole, each representing a different point of view. George Macaulay Trevelyan, the most eminent of the Whig historians, presents the Reform Bill as a precisely calculated concession, large enough to allay the revolutionary threat but moderate enough to win approval in Parliament. He gives great prominence to the possibility of violence and calls the bill the "sheet-anchor of society" in the turbulent period before its passage. Is there a paradox in his fear of popular disorder and his view of passage of the bill as a victory for sovereignty of the people? J. A. R. Marriott, in the preface to his *England Since Waterloo* notes that he has been accused of presenting a Tory version of the nineteenth century, but he denies any intended partisanship. Whether the accusation is true of the book as a whole may be a matter of dispute, but there is no doubt that his treatment of the reform controversy is Tory. His account parallels Trevelyan to a large degree in discussing the origins of the demand for reform and the danger of the period, but his emphases in discussing the bill's movement through Parliament are different. Why does he think the Tories appreciated the implications of the bill better than the Whigs? Why does he single out the House of Lords as the scene of the real conflict over reform?

The foundation work in British labor history has been done by several husband-wife teams—Sidney and Beatrice Webb, John L. and Barbara Hammond, and G. D. H. and Margaret Cole. Whether individually or in pairs, they charted the first landmarks of the subject and placed all subsequent scholars in their debt. Cole especially was attracted to the political side of the labor movement. In his "short" (three volume) history of the working-class movement he treats the Reform Bill solely from the viewpoint of the working class, although he recognizes that other groups had a stake in its outcome. To the workers he gives prime credit for its passage, although it excluded them from its benefits. Do the workers deserve the importance Cole attributes to them? Are they justified in considering the bill the betrayal of 1832?

One of the revisionists, Asa Briggs, asks what the ends were to which the reformers wanted to put the political power they sought? By examining the "geography" of discontent he shows a picture of conflicting and complementary motives more complex than one painted in broad strokes of "Whig," "Tory," "Radical," or "working class." His "sociological" approach denies us the comfort of easy generalizations.

To what extent do the differences among the historians arise from conflicting evidence on the same points and to what extent from differing emphases? Why does Trevelyan give the Whigs credit for reinterpreting the Constitution while Marriott attributes better understanding of the reform to the Tories and Cole says the workers played the leading part? And why is Briggs so guarded in his judgments on the reform?

Several of the writers in the first group of selections have called attention to the July Revolution of 1830 in France as a catalyst of the reform movement in England, a question considered in the second group. Élie Halévy, a noted French scholar and author of a six-volume history of England in the nineteenth century, is the most emphatic spokesman for this belief. He argues that this revolution moved the reform question to the center of the English political stage in the summer of 1830 and significantly influenced the Parliamentary election then in progress in favor of reform. He calls the fall of the Duke of Wellington the natural outcome of the fall of Charles X and goes so far as to suggest that there would have been no Reform Act without the July Revolution. This view of 1830 is challenged in an article by Norman Gash. Gash, a close student of the workings of politics in the fashion of Namier, looks closely at the election of 1830 for evidence of French influence. He concludes that while interest in French events was high, their effect on domestic affairs has been greatly exaggerated. Reform "was hidden in the future" in 1830 and it required "another general election to win the battle of reform." Why do the two authors read the results of the 1830 elections differently? Is Halévy inclined to see English affairs from a French perspective? Or is Gash taking the narrow attitude of a John Bull?

Regardless of whether the July Revolution was responsible for changing politicians' minds on reform, historians have long recognized that reform was won in the midst of great political flux. Party alignments, always loose during this period, had broken down completely under Wellington's government in the late 1820s. In the period that followed, the old cliché about politics making strange bedfellows became a reality as unusual partnerships were formed for and against the bill. Credit for securing passage of the bill has been variously ascribed, as is seen from the third group of readings.

In a study sympathetic to the Whigs and the Radicals, J. Salwyn Schapiro compares British and French experience in the nineteenth century and argues that England's long historical tradition of liberalism enabled the Philosophical Radicals to strike a bargain with the aristocracy. In a compromise of all the parties (except the working class!), reform forestalled revolution. What was the basis for this alliance of the Radicals of the middle class with the aristocracy? Do you agree with the weight that Schapiro gives to the intellectual factor in the outcome of reform?

Two working-class historians, G. D. H. Cole and his brother-in-law Raymond Postgate, see a different combination of support. They show a variety of groups who favored reform ranging from Whig to democratic working class, but the specific positions and interrelation of these groups remained undefined until the Grey government presented its proposals in spring 1831. Then, although there were some differences of attitude, most middle- and working-class groups saw a mutual advantage in supporting the bill. They drew even closer together following the Lords' rejection of the bill in October 1831. Faced with this determination on behalf of the bill and the threat of revolution if it failed, the Whigs pressed forward until they secured approval. How do the Schapiro and the Cole and Postgate accounts compare with respect to the role of the Benthamites? The role of revolution? Middle-class attitudes toward violence? Compare the Cole and Postgate selection with the Briggs selection. Do the discussions of middle-class and working-class roles in the reform differ?

In a revisionist account D. C. Moore challenges the equation of reform and revolution so commonly found in accounts of the Reform Bill and finds the concession theory of the bill's passage inadequate. He notes the part played by the "country Party" of former Tories who had supported Wellington before 1829 but who swung behind Grey in 1830. Pointing out the changes in the bill which strengthened their influence, he suggests that the measure may have been wrought as much by the rural gentry as the urban middle class. What evidence does he supply for the influence of the country Tories? Why did they desert Wellington after 1829? What are the implications of Moore's article for the interpretation of Schapiro and of Cole and Postgate?

The assumption central to the concession theory which Moore attacked was that England was genuinely threatened by revolution in 1831–1832. The fourth group of selections addresses this issue, which is a recurring theme in the work of writers of all four schools. J. R. M. Butler expresses it for the Whigs. Although cautious in his estimate of the situation in May 1832, he nevertheless is convinced that a carefully developed Radical plan to force the government into concession existed and would have been put into operation if the Grey government had left office during the "days of May." What is his evidence for this view? What use did the Radicals want to make of their "revolution"?

Joseph Hamburger, a political scientist who has ventured into history, believes that the danger seen by Butler was more illusory than real. Instead of a revolutionary conspiracy by the Radicals, he sees the Reform Bill agitation as an exercise in the application of a theory of orderly political change developed by the Benthamite James Mill several years before. By a calculated propaganda campaign involving the manipulation of mass organization and an alarmist press, the Radicals played on the Whigs' fear of revolution without actually having to risk it. The Reform Act was the mark of their success. Do you see any similarities between Hamburger's account and that of Schapiro? What effect does Hamburger's interpretation of nonrevolution have on the other authors' estimates of the Whigs? The middle class? The working class?

A totally different explanation of why Britain escaped revolution comes from Élie Halévy. As a Frenchman contrasting the experience of his own country with that of England, he finds the answer to the question in evangelical religion, especially Methodism. In a general assessment of England's condition in 1815 he argues that John Wesley's commitment to the established political order had been absorbed by his Methodist followers and, through a sympathetic spirit, by the Nonconformist sects. Thus in the years that followed 1815 England was deprived of the revolutionary bourgeois and working class leadership so important elsewhere. Halévy's interpretation has been questioned by other historians, among them Robert F. Wearmouth, a student of the influence of Methodism on the nineteenth-century English working class. While conceding the political conservatism of *Weslayan* Methodism, he suggests that other Methodist groups were inclined to democratic political action and that the Methodist system of class organization provided a model widely copied by radical groups in the 1830s. Can you explain the conflict in the interpretations of these two authors? What relation do their views suggest between spiritual movements and social and political action in history?

The last group of selections presents the views of the four schools on the aftereffects of reform. They differ on the meaning of the Reform Act for the period that followed, as they differ on the bill's progress through Parliament. A nineteenth-century Whig historian, Justin McCarthy, applauds the bill for establishing important constitutional principles capable of further development. Treating the act as an imperfect compromise that was nevertheless the first important step, he speaks of the habit of the English people to lay in a stock of reform which they allow nearly to run out before replenishing the store.

An extreme statement of the Tory position, full of nostalgia for the past, comes from O. F. Christie. Writing of the Tory reasons for fear of the future in 1832, he suggests that they may not have been far wrong. He does not explicitly endorse a concept of rule by the aristocracy, but he comes very close in lamenting the vices of democracy. What does he mean when he suggests that the Reform Act "broke the Constitution"?

Combining an interest in the working class with a desire to trace the formation of distinct social classes in English society, E. P. Thompson believes that passage of the Reform Bill completed the process of establishing a working-class identity and awareness of interests in opposition to those of other groups. Chartism began "at the moment when the Reform Bill received the Royal Assent," and a "collective self-consciousness" marks working-class activity in the years that followed. Why does Thompson see such sharp class delineations in politics after 1832?

The last selection is a review by W. L. Burn of a book by a revisionist whom we have already encountered. Norman Gash's study of postreform electoral politics, published in 1953, analyzes the effect of the provisions of the Reform Act and presents in great detail the means by which constituency elections were conducted in the two decades following its passage. This review, which incorporates much of Gash's work, discusses politics under reform with much sensitivity and a moderate Tory bent. Burn forces us to ask how much change in the basic political process the Reform Act really made? Can it be called a victory for one interest or another?

"Upon the matter of regulating the suffrage," wrote Montesquieu, "depends the destruction or salvation of states." All the authors of the selections given here believe the Reform Act was a critical event in English history because of the changes it made in the suffrage and representation. Yet they differ on whether the salvation or the destruction of British institutions hinged on the outcome of the controversy. Their discussions raise two basic questions: Was revolution really possible in England in 1831–1832? If so, by what means was it avoided? In order to answer these questions, the reader will need to ask others. Is there something unique about England's historical experience—a "good genius" as Trevelyan has called it—which enabled its people to meet this crisis? Were domestic institutions and the mechanisms of order stable enough to withstand attack if it had been made? What was the relation of Parliament and people in the resolution of the crisis? What relation should we see between the Reform Bill agitation and earlier and later British Radicalism? Do we delude ourselves when we compare British reform with Continental revolution? Questions of broader scope arise also. What can English reform experience tell us of the process of political change in a rapidly developing society? Were the events unique or can they tell us something useful for understanding other countries in other times, including our own?

The reader will not find the answers to all of his questions here. He can only begin to untangle the complexities of a great historical event and to see why historians looking at the same happenings interpret them differently.

In the reprinted selections footnotes appearing in the original sources have in general been omitted unless they contribute to the argument or better understanding of the selection.

GEORGE MACAULAY TREVELYAN (1876–1962),
grand-nephew of the great Whig historian Thomas
Babington Macaulay, was for many years Regius
Professor of Modern History at Cambridge University.
A much honored historian, his work covers the
span of English history, but nineteenth-century
reforms and reformers held a special attraction for
him, as his books, *Lord Grey of the Reform Bill* and
The Life of John Bright, bear witness. In this
selection he celebrates the continuity of British
history and institutions and considers the Reform Act
as an outstanding example of the special English
talent for moderate change. In an account concerned
primarily with Parliamentary political maneuvers,
he presents a characteristic Whig view of how the
concession of reform was wrung from a reluctant
aristocracy.*

► *Reform Wrung from the Tories*

The genius of the English people for
politics was faced by new problems arising out of those which it had solved of
old. The age of the Tudors had seen the
destruction of the mediaeval privileges
of Church and Baronage, that had prevented the unity and progress of the nation; in their place the full sovereignty
of the Crown in Parliament had been
established. Under the Stuarts, Parliament had won the supremacy in its partnership with the Crown, while the principle of local government had been preserved against despotic encroachment.
In the eighteenth century, Parliament
had acquired executive efficiency
through the Cabinet system. These institutions were England's unique and

native heritage. But they were administered by a privileged group of borough
owners, magistrates and members of
close corporations, roughly identified in
sympathy with the country gentlemen,
but not co-extensive even with that
class. This group had by long possession
come to regard their own monopoly as
synonymous with the Constitution itself. To speak ill of the rotten boroughs
and close corporations was to utter
"seditious" words against our "matchless
Constitution." But in spite of Lord
Eldon and those who thought with him,
Parliament, Cabinet and local government had been created by England's
practical imagination in the past, and
had now by a fresh creative process to

* From G. M. Trevelyan, *British History in the Ninteenth Century and After* (London: Longmans, Green & Co., Ltd., 1937), pp. 224–28, 230–31, 235–39, Reprinted by permission of Longmans,
Green & Co., Ltd., and David McKay Company, Inc.

be adapted to the needs of a new type of society born of the Industrial Revolution. . . .

To the Whigs between 1830 and 1835 belongs the credit of destroying the monopoly, reinterpreting the Constitution, and harnessing public opinion to the machine of government. Whatever some of the Whigs might say about the "finality" of their Bill, this new principle, when once admitted, could brook no limitation until complete democracy had been realised under old English forms. On the other hand the belief of the anti-Reform Tories that the Reform Bill would lead at once to the overthrow of Crown and Lords, Church and property, was the exact reverse of the truth. It was due to the Bill that England was not involved in the vicious circle of continental revolution and reaction, and that our political life kept its Anglo-Saxon moorings.

Both the Liberal-Tories in Canning's day, and the Whig followers of Grey and Althorp, were acting under the direct inspiration of middle-class opinion, and under compelling fear of working-class revolt.

. . . The movement of Parliamentary Reform was revived in the nineteenth century first of all by the working-men, because their economic misery was the most acute. The middle classes had been divided or indifferent during the radical agitation of the Peterloo time. The Whigs, meanwhile, to prevent division in their own ranks, waited on the middle-class lead, Lord Grey always abiding by his declaration of 1810 that he would again move for Reform when, but only when, the English people had taken it up "seriously and affectionately." In the year 1830 he saw his condition fulfilled. The middle classes, in whom he read public opinion, took up Reform "seriously and affectionately";

whereupon, greatly to the surprise of friends and foes, the old nobleman was as good as his word.

There were many reasons why the middle classes moved rapidly towards Parliamentary Reform in the three years following Canning's death. The removal of the statesman whom so many had begun to regard as the national leader, threw them back into their former attitude of opposition to Government, and the reversal of his foreign policy by Wellington was a sharp reminder that only Parliamentary Reform could secure that national affairs should be continuously guided on popular lines.

Meanwhile any avenue of escape through "bit by bit" reform was closed by the action of the Parliamentary Tories in 1828, when they refused to allow the seats of certain boroughs disfranchised for peculiarly gross corruption to be given to the unrepresented cites of Manchester and Birmingham. It was on that issue that Huskisson, Palmerston and Melbourne had left Wellington's Ministry, and the event made a deep impression on public opinion.

In January 1830 Thomas Attwood founded the Birmingham Political Union, to agitate for a large but undefined measure of Parliamentary Reform. It was, professedly and actually, a union of middle and working classes; it was the first step towards their co-operation in Radical politics which marked the Victorian era. In other industrial centres, such as Manchester, it was more difficult for employers and workmen to co-operate, though both were now avowed enemies of the "borough-mongers."

Bad trade and hard times had returned. Common economic misery sharpened the sense of common political wrongs, and predisposed the whole nation to unite in the demand for Reform. In 1830 Cobbett enjoyed a second period of great popular influence, which he used as he had used his popularity in 1817, to turn all streams of discontent into the one channel of Parliamentary Reform. But whereas in 1817 he had been the leader of the working class alone, he found in 1830 that even the farmers thronged to hear him speak, as he rode on his cob from one market-town to another. Radicalism had become for the moment almost a national creed.

There were differences of opinion as to the economic cure for the distress of the time. Some, like Attwood, saw it in currency reform; more, like Cobbett, in retrenchment; others in Free Trade; others in Factory Acts or in Socialism. But all were agreed that reform of Parliament was the necessary first step before anything effective could be done.

The greatest danger to the cause of Reform arose from dissension as to what the new franchise ought to be. Some claimed household suffrage, others desired government by "the solid and respectable part of the community." But the rallying cry of "Down with the rotten boroughs" served to harmonise these discords. Every class that was hoping to exert greater influence over Parliament was enraged that more than half the House of Commons owed their seats to individual peers or commoners. The borough owners, who for generations back had pulled the strings of ministerial favour and lived on the fat of patronage—they and their kinsmen and their servants—suddenly found themselves objects of universal execration, and the "borough property" which they had inherited or purchased denounced as having been stolen from the nation. The cry against the "borough-

mongers" rose on every side. Capitalists, clerks, shopkeepers, besides that great majority of the inhabitants who were comprised under the two categories of working-men and Dissenters, all were talking against "Old Corruption." The very ostlers and publicans entered into the spirit of the hour. Even country gentlemen who did not happen to have an "interest" in a borough, began to think that they would like to see a fairer proportion of county members in the House, honestly chosen by themselves and their farmers. The only class that remained solid for the old system was the Church clergy, who were so conscious of unpopularity that they believed Reform would lead to the destruction of the Establishment.

Into the midst of a society thus agitated came the news of the Paris revolution of 1830, the glorious days of July." Charles X and his minister Polignac had provoked their own downfall by illegally suspending the Constitution. Although the fighting on the barricades had been done by the workmen, the movement was not permitted to turn "red," but solidified round Lafayette, the National Guard and the *bourgeois* King, Louis Philippe. The *noblesse* and the Clericals had fallen once more, but property was safe. These events could not, like the French Revolutions of 1792 and 1848, and the Commune of 1871, be used as a warning against change over here. The year 1830 still stands as the one occasion when the French set a political example that influenced us otherwise than by repulsion.

The first effect of the inspiring news from France was to increase the number of open seats carried by the Opposition in the General Election that August. A new Parliament had to be elected, on account of the death of George and the accession of William IV, the popular sailor king. It was the House of Commons chosen in these circumstances that turned out Wellington and carried the Reform Bill by one vote. Brougham, the interpreter between the official Whigs and the national movement for Reform, was sent up as a member for Yorkshire, amid the rejoicings of the whole country. He never again touched such a height of popular influence.

But the French Revolution of 1830 did more than affect the elections. It gave Englishmen the sense of living in a new era, when great changes could safely be made. To act boldly on behalf of the people, it was seen, did not produce anarchy as the Tories had argued ever since 1789. Rather, it was half-measures that were dangerous, and resistance to the people that was fatal. Our middle class saw the *bourgeoisie* governing France, and blushed that in England they themselves were still subject to an aristocracy. The working-men heard that the *ouvriers* had defeated the Army in fair fight, and the word went round that what Frenchmen had done Englishmen could do at need. Pamphlets on the technique of street-fighting had a suggestive popularity. The knowledge that Englishmen were so thinking, and that Frenchmen had so acted, gravely affected the politics of the propertied class as a whole, and not a few of the borough owners themselves, persuading them to make concessions they would never have dreamt of two years before. . . .

All autumn the agitation in the country was deeper than political. Economic misery, pauperism, starvation and class injustice had brought society to the verge of dissolution. Rick-burning, under the orders of "Captain Swing," that dark abstraction of the vengeance of the ruined peasantry, kept the rural

south in terror. In the industrial north the workmen were drilling and preparing for social war. The middle classes clamoured for Reform, equally to pacify the revolutionary spirit below, and to secure their own rights against an aristocracy they had ceased to trust.

In the first fortnight of November, when Wellington met the recently elected Parliament, came the most important political crisis of the century. Everyone was looking to the new House of Commons to save the country, yet no one knew what it would do, even in making its choice between Wellington and Grey. The group system still prevailed, and many of the groups had no defined political allegiance. As late as November the First, there were three future Prime Ministers waiting to find out whether they were Whig or Tory; for the Canningites under Lords Melbourne and Palmerston, and the independent group led by Edward Stanley, "the Rupert of Debate," came up pledged to moderate Reform and looking to see whether Wellington or Grey would give them what they wanted. If the Duke had made a declaration promising a peaceful and liberal policy towards France and Belgium, and a small measure of Parliamentary Reform, he could have rallied these men round him and stayed in office. It is indeed unlikely that a Tory Reform Bill would have been large enough to pacify the country. But in any case the experiment was not destined to be tried.

The King's speech mentioned the Belgian revolution with ominous disapproval, and when Lord Grey called attention to the absence of any promise of Reform, the Duke replied that "the system of representation possessed the full and entire confidence of the country."

The Duke had challenged the nation,

and the nation took up the challenge. The excitement inside Parliament was a feeble reflection of the feeling outside; yet never were the lobbies and clubs more busy, or busy to better purpose. In a week the basis had been laid of the Whig-Liberal party that was to dominate the next generation. The Canningites and moderate reformers all enlisted under Grey's banner, and were prepared to join a Whig Government on the programme of "Peace, Retrenchment and Reform." With the help of a few High Tories who were still so anxious to be revenged on the Duke for Catholic Emancipation that they cared not what happened afterwards, the Government was beaten in the Commons on the Civil List. Wellington resigned, and the King sent for Lord Grey. . . .

At the very moment of the change of Ministry, the labourers of the southern counties, driven by famine, were marching through the countryside demanding a living wage of half a crown a day. They were cruelly punished at the assizes, when 450 of the rioters were torn from their families and transported to Australia, besides three unjustly executed. The new Whig Ministers, in a panic lest the propertied classes should confound "Reform" with "Jacobinism and disorder," would not mitigate these sentences. In connection with the same riots they prosecuted Richard Carlile and Cobbett for articles in the Press. Cobbett at his trial in the following July, made the Whigs look as foolish before a British jury as the Tories of old. His acquittal effectually discouraged a revival of that spirit of coercion which Peel as Home Secretary had so wisely abandoned.

The Whigs had made a bad start. But when on March 1, 1831, Lord John Russell introduced the Reform Bill into the Commons, and revealed the well-kept secret that all the "nomination" boroughs were to be abolished without compensation to the borough-owners, Ministers sprang to the summit of popularity at a single bound. The Tories were dumfounded. They had confidently expected a weak measure, buying up a few of the rotten borough seats to give them to a few great cities; such a Bill would have left the nation cold and the reformers divided; lacking support from outside, it could pass the Houses only by agreement, after being further whittled down; finally the Whigs would be turned out as incompetent sciolists and power would revert to its long-tried possessors. But instead of lending themselves to this plan, Ministers had summoned the whole nation to their support, to overawe the recusants at Westminster. The bold appeal was not merely a winning move in the political game, but it established the fundamental principle of the "new constitution," namely, that in the last resort the opinion of the nation was to count for more than the opinion of the legislators. . . .

A defeat in Committee soon narrowed the issue to a choice between a new Ministry with a much modified Bill, or a General Election to save Bill and Ministry together. In such circumstances a modern Prime Minister could claim a dissolution of Parliament as of right. But under George III and his sons dissolution was, in custom as well as in law, a personal prerogative of the king. Would William dissolve at Grey's request? The decisive crisis in the fortunes of the Bill had come, and the choice lay with a retired admiral of no great brains or experience in affairs of State, but with an instinct of personal loyalty to his Ministers which sharply distinguished him from his father and brother before him.

In January 1831, while the draft Bill had been a secret between William and his confidential servants, Grey had persuaded his master to allow him to introduce it—a permission necessary under the custom of the Constitution as George III had defined it. Grey had persuaded the King that the Bill was an "aristocratical" measure, designed to save the Constitution from more revolutionary changes. And so it was in Grey's mind. Its "democratical" implications only began to be apparent to William after it had become public, when the joy of the Radicals of whom he lived in terror, and the rage of the Tories with whom he lived in intimacy, gradually made him realise what he had done. In April he had to decide whether he would accept Grey's resignation or his advice to dissolve. The straw that weighed down the balance in his mind was the fact that there had been a majority of one for the second reading. With many misgivings he granted Grey his dissolution.

The General Election was almost as onesided and enthusiastic, so far as popular opinion was concerned, as the elections for the Restoration Parliament. The Reformers carried almost all the open constituencies, including seventy-four English county seats out of eighty. But no amount of popular intimidation could shake the hold of the proprietors on the nomination seats. In their last Parliament the rotten borough members voted two to one against the Bill, in much the same numbers as before the election.

But there was now a majority of 136 for the Bill. It passed through the Commons that summer under Lord Althorp's patient management in Committee, and went up to the Lords, where it was thrown out on second reading by a majority of forty-one votes....

A single false step by the Ministers might have precipitated anarchy. The Army, smaller than at any other period in our modern annals, was insufficient to keep order in England and Scotland, in addition to its usual task in Ireland. Peel's police as yet only existed in London. It was impossible to raise volunteer forces to put down Reform mobs. The workmen in the North were drilling and arming to fight the Lords. In the South the ricks were blazing night after night. Unemployment and starvation urged desperate deeds. The first visitation of cholera added to the gloom and terror of the winter of 1831–2.

Employers and City men clamoured more loudly every week for a creation of peers to pass the Bill and save social order. The working classes, if it came to blows, would fight not for this Bill of the Ten Pound householders, but for a Bill that enfranchised their own class, and for much else besides. Civil strife, if it came, might easily degenerate into a war between "haves" and "have-nots." The Bill seemed the sheet-anchor of society. Even the burning of the central part of Bristol by Radical ruffians failed to cause a serious reaction, each side drawing its own moral from the event.

Grey kept his head. He neither resigned nor, as the King urged, whittled down the Bill. On the other hand he refused, in spite of the remonstrance of the leading members of his Cabinet, to force the King to a premature decision about peer-making, before the time came when circumstances would be too strong for William's reluctance.

Before Christmas a new Bill was introduced, modified in detail to meet some reasonable criticisms and so save the face of the "waverers" among the peers, but not weakened as a democratic measure. It quickly passed the Commons, and was accepted by nine votes on the second reading in the Lords.

The final crisis, known as the "Days of May," was provoked by an attempt of the Lords to take the Bill out of the hands of the Ministers in charge, and amend it in their own way. This was countered by the resignation of the Cabinet. Resignation in the previous autumn, when the Lords had thrown the Bill right out, would have produced anarchy. Now it secured and hastened the last stages of a journey of which the goal was already in sight. In October 1831 the country, taken by surprise by the Lords' action, was not properly organised, as the riots had shown. But in May 1832, the Political Unions had the situation in hand. Grey's resignation was not followed by violence or rioting, but by a silent and formidable preparation for ultimate resistance in case he did not speedily return. The English genius for local self-government, voluntary combination and self-help, which had little or no expression in the close municipalities, found its outlet in these unofficial Political Unions of citizens determined alike on order and on freedom.[1] These organisations, improvised by the British people, constituted the

strongest proof of its fitness to work self-governing institutions of a more official character. Abhorred by the King and Tories who clamoured for their suppression, the Unions were tolerated by the Whig Ministers on the condition of their ceasing to arm and drill.

Grey had resigned because the King refused to create peers. But William was now prepared to do anything short of that to get the Bill through intact. He appealed to Wellington to form a Tory Ministry for the purpose of carrying "the Bill, the whole Bill and nothing but the Bill" through the House of Lords—on the precedent of Catholic Emancipation three years before. The most fearless, if not always the wisest, of public servants accepted this extraordinary commission, the nature of which was not understood in the country, where people naturally supposed that the victor of Waterloo, who had pronounced against all Reform, was coming back to rule them by the sword. If Wellington had succeeded in forming a Ministry, the Political Unions would have led resistance, with what result it is impossible to say. But the actual cause of the Duke's abandoning the task was not his fear of popular resistance, but the refusal of Peel and the Tories in the House of Commons to take part in a scheme so absurd and dangerous, no longer with a hope of modifying the Bill, but solely to save the face of the Lords. The King was obliged to come to terms with Grey, and could only get him back by a written promise to create any number of peers necessary to carry the Bill. The threat when known in the Upper House sufficed, and the Reform Bill became law.

---

[1] They had been formed in most towns. The model of Attwood's Birmingham Union, presided over by middle-class leaders, but including all classes, prevailed in the midlands and west. In the industrial north there were "low Political Unions" of working-men only. In some towns there were both kinds of Political Union formed side by side.

In a long career JOHN A. R. MARRIOTT (1859–1945) combined both academic life and politics. He was educated at Oxford and taught there for many years, holding a fellowship much of the time at Worcester College. He contested Rochdale's seat in Parliament unsuccessfully as a Conservative in 1886, but sat as a Conservative member of Parliament for Oxford City from 1917 to 1922 and for York from 1923 to 1929. His long list of books includes works on Italy, Germany, England, France, and diplomatic history. In this selection from a text on nineteenth-century England he reviews many of the events related by Trevelyan, but he offers a more sympathetic treatment of Tory resistance to reform.*

▶ ||| *Tory Reluctance Justified*

The supreme issue between parties at this moment was that of parliamentary reform. It was, therefore, appropriate that on the resignation of Wellington and Peel the formation of the new Ministry should be entrusted to Earl Grey. Born in 1764, the scion of an ancient Northumbrian house, and the eldest son of a distinguished soldier, he entered the House of Commons as Member for his native county in 1786. In 1792 he became the most influential spokesman of the *Society of Friends of the People,* and thence onwards for forty years was the foremost advocate of parliamentary reform. In 1792, 1793, and 1797 he had brought forward motions in the House of Commons, only to encounter a solid phalanx of opposition inspired to reaction by the dread example of France. But despite his long political career Lord Grey had little administrative experience. Less than two years at the Admiralty and the Foreign Office (1806–1807) represented the sum of his official life. Nevertheless, he was obviously marked out as the chief of a "Reform" Ministry, and the King's choice merely ratified general expectation. . . .

The situation which confronted Lord Grey's Ministry was not devoid of difficulty. In Ireland O'Connell had already unfurled the flag of "Repeal," and the troops had been called out (Oct. 1830) to suppress the disturbances which

* From J. A. R. Marriott, *England Since Waterloo* (London: Methuen & Co., Ltd., 1913), pp. 89–91, 95–101. Reprinted by permission of Methuen & Co., Ltd., and Barnes & Noble, Inc. Footnotes omitted.

marked the inauguration of the new agitation. In England there were ominous signs of a recrudescence of the recent epidemic of social disorder. Luddites and rick-burners were again to the fore. "Every post," writes Greville, "brings fresh accounts of conflagrations, destruction of machinery, association of labourers, and compulsory rise of wages. Cobbett and Carlile write and harangue to inflame the minds of the people, who are already set in motion and excited by all the events which have happened abroad." The new Ministry had not been in office two days before they found it necessary to issue a proclamation offering large rewards for the discovery of "offenders, rioters, or burners," and promising all the Lord Lieutenants assistance in the suppression of disorder. Hampshire, Wilts, Berkshire, and Buckingham were particularly conspicuous for crime and disturbance, and in December no less than 1,000 rioters, 700 of whom came from Hants and Wilts, were brought to trial before a Special Commission at Winchester. In January Carlile was convicted at the Old Bailey of "addressing inflammatory language to the labouring classes," and was sentenced to two years' imprisonment and a fine of £200. Cobbett, arraigned on a similar charge, escaped punishment owing to the postponement of his trial for six months. By that time the panic caused by agrarian disorder had abated, and public interest was concentrated upon the fate of the Reform Bill.

For some large measure of parliamentary reform the time was clearly ripe. It is true that there had been in recent years some slackening in the intensity of the demand. For whereas the year 1821 had produced a crop of nineteen petitions in favour of reform and the year 1823 no less than twenty-nine, the years between 1824 and 1829

had produced none at all. Commercial prosperity is a sure solvent of political agitation. But by 1830 prosperity was once more waning, and interest in purely political questions was quickened by the outbreak of revolution in France. In July the legitimist Monarchy, which had been restored by the bayonets of the allies in 1815, finally tottered to its fall; Charles X was drive into exile, and Louis Philippe, Duke of Orleans, thanks mainly to the support of the Parisian bourgeoisie, was installed as "the Citizen King." The shock thus given to the principle of legitimacy was felt in greater or less degree in most of the European States, in Poland, Italy, Germany, and most of all in Belgium. Great Britain felt it least, but even here it gave renewed impulse to the cry for parliamentary reform. . . .

Throughout the autumn and winter of 1830–1831 there was a continuous agitation in favour of reform. The seed sown in many soils during the last half-century was rapidly ripening for harvest. The philosophical radicalism of the Utilitarians; the work of Bentham, of James and John Stuart Mill, of Hume and others; the democratic liberalism of Francis Place; the communism of Robert Owen, all these were bearing fruit in the ferment of opinion and the political organization which immediately preceded the Reform Bill of 1831.

The first work of the Grey Ministry was to appoint a Committee to draft a Bill to "amend the representation of the people in England and Wales." The Committee consisted of two members of the Cabinet: Lord Durham and Sir James Graham; Lord Duncannon, the chief Government Whip, and Lord John Russell. To these, as they were approaching the end of their labours, the Duke of Richmond was added. Creevey declares that of the Bill, which is known to history as his, Lord Grey "knew not one syllable till it was presented to him all ready cut and dry." This myth has been finally exposed by the publication of Graham's Memorandum on the proceedings in the Committee of Four. The original draft proposed by the Committee was substantially amended by the Cabinet who (1) struck out the vote by ballot; (2) retained septennial as against quinquennial Parliaments; and (3) substituted £10 for the proposed £20 rating qualification in boroughs.

On March 1st Lord John Russell, though not yet a member of the Cabinet, laid the ministerial proposals before the House of Commons. They proved to be more drastic than even the most sanguine Radicals had dared to hope. The first feature of the Bill was a large measure of disfranchisement. Sixty boroughs with less than 2,000 inhabitants apiece, returning in the aggregate 119 members, were to be totally disfranchised; the united boroughs of Weymouth and Melcombe Regis were to lose two of their four members; 47 other boroughs, with more than 2,000 but less than 4,000 inhabitants, were to lose one member apiece. Thus 168 seats were placed at the disposal of the Government. Enfranchisement was on an adequate but less generous scale. Seven of the largest unrepresented towns like Manchester and Birmingham were to get 2 members apiece; twenty more were to get 1; the London boroughs to get 8; 57 were to go to the English counties; 3 to Ireland, 5 to Scotland, and 1 to Wales. The nett reduction in the numbers of the House was to be 62. As to voting qualification there was an immense simplification. In the boroughs there was to be a £10 rating qualification, and freemen were to retain their votes. In the counties, copyholders and £50 tenants were added to the old 40s. freeholders. The Bill passed the second reading by a majority of only one. Before it was committed General Gascoyne carried, by a majority of eight, an instruction that there should be no diminution in the total number of representatives of England and Wales. On this rebuff the Ministry decided upon an immediate appeal to the country; on April 22nd Parliament was dissolved in hot haste by the King, and amid the wildest excitement a General Election was held. The issue was as nearly isolated as it ever can be in English politics. "The Bill, the whole Bill, and nothing but the Bill," was the rallying cry of the Whigs. Their triumph was complete, and they came back with a majority of more than a hundred. The Reform Bill, with only a few minor changes, was reintroduced by Lord John Russell on June 24th, and on July 7th it was read a second time by a majority of 136 (367 to 231). The Tories fought it for two months in Committee, but before the end of September it was sent up to the Lords backed by a majority substantially undiminished. The Lords, after nearly a week's debate, threw it out (Oct. 8th) by a majority of 41 (199 to 158).

The action of the Lords is said to have brought the country to the verge of revolution. There were serious riots in several of the large towns, notably in Derby, Nottingham, Worcester, Coventry, and—most serious of all—in Bristol. It is difficult to believe that these were the work of the classes about to be enfranchised. The Reform Bill, however, was looked upon only as an instalment. The political principle once admitted was to be the lever for far-reaching social and economic change. Behind the Utilitarians were the Owenites. Social revolution was to come in the wake of political reform. The Whigs might persuade themselves that a measure so generous and comprehensive would be accepted by all parties as a final settlement. The Tories knew better; so did the Radicals; the Chartists best of all. Not otherwise can we explain the disturbances in the autumn of 1831. Commercial and agricultural distress and the dread of pestilence[1] doubtless added fuel to the flames, but the conflagration was due to a mass of economic and social discontent which had been accumulating during the last half-century. That discontent found . . . cold comfort in the clauses of the Act of 1832. But the immediate cry was for "the Bill."

Parliament was reopened on December 6th. A week later Lord John Russell introduced his third Reform Bill, this time in a shape considerably altered. The disfranchisement clauses were decidedly less rigorous, and were based not only on the principle of population, but upon the number of inhabited houses, and the contribution of the town to the assessed taxes. More important still, the numbers of the House were to remain unchanged. The Bill passed rapidly through all its stages in the House of Commons, and before the end of March was launched upon its perilous voyage in the Lords.

Would the ship reach port safely? In no responsible quarter was it believed that the Lords would yield without coercion, or the certain prospect of its application. If they gave the Bill a second reading it would only be with the intention of emasculating it in Committee. Under these circumstances some of the Cabinet were in favour of obtaining from the King an immediate guarantee that he would assent if necessary to the creation of a sufficient number of Peers to carry the Bill. The King, however, demurred; Lord Grey himself was re-

[1] Cholera appeared in November.

luctant, and the majority of the Cabinet decided to await events. In the Lords, thanks mainly to the attitude of the "waverers," the Bill was read a second time (April 14th) by a majority of nine (184 to 175). But on May 7th Lord Lyndhurst carried by a large majority (151 to 116) a motion in favour of postponing the clauses (with Schedule A) dealing with the disfranchisement of the smallest boroughs, until the rest of the Bill had been approved. The situation foreseen by Lord Durham, Sir James Graham, and other "stalwarts" in the Cabinet had actually arisen, and the Cabinet now advised the King to create as many Peers "as might ensure the success of the Bill in all its essential principles." The King, though in favour of extensive reform, was strongly opposed on principle to the coercion of the Peers, and regretfully accepted the proffered resignation of the Ministry. The House of Commons expressed its confidence in the retiring Ministry by a large majority, and the country was profoundly agitated by the crisis. The King turned to Lord Lyndhurst, to Manners-Sutton (then Speaker of the House of Commons), and to the Duke of Wellington. Neither Lyndhurst nor Manners-Sutton could form a Ministry, but the Duke was willing to try in order "to save the Sovereign from the indignity of having so gross a violation of the Constitution imposed upon him." But everything really depended upon Peel. No Ministry could now avoid a large measure of "Reform." Not even to save the King and the Lords was Peel prepared to pledge himself to this. Negotiations broke down, and on May 14th the Duke advised the King to recall Lord Grey. For his own part the Duke promised that "in order to save His Majesty's personal honour as to the creation of Peers . . . he would . . . remove all pretence for such a creation by withdrawing his opposition." Greville's appreciation of the personal conduct of the two leading actors in this episode is not very wide of the mark. "Peel acted right from bad motives, the Duke wrong from good ones." The Grey Ministry was reinstated, and the King in writing granted permission to Earl Grey "and to his Chancellor Lord Brougham to create such a number of Peers as will be sufficient to ensure the passing of the Reform Bill, first calling up Peers' eldest sons." The battle was won. The opponents of the Bill in the House of Lords withdrew, and on June 7th the Bill received the Royal assent. The same session witnessed the passing of similar Bills for the reform of the representation in Scotland and Ireland.

The changes effected by this legislation in its final shape may now be summarized. First, as regards disfranchisement: 56 boroughs with less than 2,000 inhabitants were totally disfranchised. Of these 55 had two members each; one, Higham Ferrers, had one; Weymouth and Melcombe Regis lost two of their four members; and 30 boroughs with less than 4,000 inhabitants lost one of their two members. Thus 143 seats were surrendered. These were redistributed as follows: 65 to English and Welsh counties; 44 to twenty-two English boroughs (two each); 21 to single member boroughs; 8 to Scotland and 5 to Ireland. The total numbers therefore remained unchanged at 658. In the boroughs a uniform £10 household franchise was established, with the reservation of the rights of resident freemen in corporate towns. In the counties the old 40s. freeholders were reinforced by copyholders and long leaseholders, and by tenants-at-will paying a rent of £50 a year. In Scotland the county franchise was given to all owners of property of £10 a year and to certain leaseholders; in Ireland to owners as in England and £20 occupiers.

The final and total result was the addition of some 455,000 electors to the roll—an addition which more than tripled the electorate. In the towns political power was vested mainly in the merchants, manufacturers, and shopkeepers; in the counties in the landowners and the farmers. In addition to the clauses defining the franchise and the distribution of seats, the Act of 1832 provided for the formation of a register of voters, for the division of constituencies into convenient polling districts, and for the restriction of the polling to two successive days.

That the Reform Acts of 1832 constituted a great political and parliamentary achievement will be denied by none. Before, however, an attempt is made to estimate its real and permanent significance, a few words may be said as to the part played in the struggle by individuals.

Throughout the whole crisis the King's behaviour was, by general consent, admirable. Not only was his conduct entirely "correct" in the constitutional sense, but "he bestowed much time and thought in going over every part of the plan, examined its bearings, asked most sensible questions." Lord Grey himself bore similar testimony: "the King's noble conduct is indeed a just theme for praise, and entitles him to all our gratitude and all our zeal in his service." To the general principles of the Bill he gave a cordial assent; as to the means by which it was forced through one branch of the legislature he had grave misgivings. How far they were justified is still a matter of controversy. In the Commons the lion's share of the work fell to Lord John Russell, ably supported by Lord Althorp, but in the Cabinet they were strongly backed both by Graham and Lord Durham.

But neither the King's closet, nor the Cabinet, nor the Commons was the scene of the real conflict over reform. The key to the position was in the House of Lords. It was the Lords, not the Monarchy nor the Commons, who were fighting for their political lives. For a century and a half the Peers—partly in their own chamber, still more through their nominees in the Lower House—had been the real rulers of England. In 1832 they were called upon to surrender a trust which they had administered, on the whole, with conspicuous fidelity and success, albeit by methods which the public opinion of to-day regards as indefensible. That they were blind to the new forces—political, social, and economical—which the last half-century had generated may be imputed to them for stupidity, but not for unrighteousness. Nor can it be denied that their estimate of the results to be apprehended from reform was nearer the mark than that of their opponents. Lord Grey himself represented his proposals as "aristocratic"; his colleagues hoped that an "effectual check would be opposed to the restless spirit of innovation"; the Whigs generally believed that the Bill was at once "conservative" and final in its terms. Nothing would have amazed them more than to learn that they were opening the flood-gates to the tide of democracy. "Neither the Whig aristocracy who introduced the first Reform Bill," says a philosophical writer, "nor the middle class whose agitation forced it through, conceived it to be even implicitly a revolutionary measure. The power of the Crown and of the House of Lords were to be maintained intact; the House of Commons was to be more representative, but not more democratic than before. The change was regarded as one of detail, not of principle; in no sense a subversion of the Constitution, but merely its adaptation to new conditions." The Duke of Wellington judged it far more shrewdly: "there is no man who considers what the Government of King, Lords, and Commons is, and the details of the manner in which it is carried on, who must not see that Government will become impracticable when the three branches shall be separate, each independent of the other, and uncontrolled in its action by any of the existing influences." It is true that the full force of the shock administered in 1832 was not felt for at least two generations. Despite organic change, the Government of England continued to be aristocratic in personnel at least until 1867. Nevertheless, it is a sound instinct which assigns to 1832 the real point of transition from Aristocracy to Democracy. The changes of 1867 and 1884 were implicit in the earlier revolution. That these changes were neither foreseen nor intended by Lord Grey and his colleagues is true, but it is nothing to the point. They opened the gates; the capture of the citadel was merely a question of time.

The instinct, therefore, which led the Lords to resist to the last the proposals of reform was, from their own point of view, perfectly sound. With the passage of the Bill their political death-warrant was signed. That an "extensive measure" could have been much longer deferred few people on either side believed, and events have more than justified the general belief.

Like Marriott, G. D. H. COLE (1889–1959) combined an academic career with active political life. Following completion of his degree at Oxford he held several appointments at the University including the Chichele Professorship of Social and Political Theory from 1944 until his retirement in 1957. Cole served first as chairman and then for many years as president of the Fabian Society and was a frequent contributor to the *New Statesman*. A voluminous and versatile writer, his work ranges over labor history, politics, political theory, economics, sociology, biography, and mysteries. In many of his works he was joined by his wife Margaret. He drew particular attention to working class participation in politics and the development of the Labour Party. In this selection he emphasizes the reform movement outside of Parliament more than the two previous writers, and he argues that the working class played the decisive role in winning reform.*

Working-class Support Decisive

Meanwhile the movement for the reform of Parliament was speedily gathering force. The House of Commons up to 1832 not only made no pretence of being a democratic body, but was hardly, in any ordinary sense of the word, a representative assembly. The most that could be claimed for it was that it "virtually represented" the classes which had a stake in the country —in other words, that it represented property rather than persons. The distribution of seats bore no proportion either to population or even to the number of electors. In 1780, the ninety-two members for the counties were returned by 130,000 voters—the county freeholders; whereas the 421 members who sat for towns and universities were returned by only 84,000 electors. Moreover, whereas the county elections did, in most cases, give at least the gentry some opportunity of expressing their views, the majority of the borough elections were pure farce. . . .

The Reform Movement, which arose between 1769 and 1780, was crushed by the terrors aroused by the Revolution in France. Thenceforth all proposals for reform were denounced as Jacobinism

* From G. D. H. Cole, *A Short History of the British Working Class Movement, 1789–1927* (London: George Allen & Unwin, Ltd., 1927), vol. 1, pp. 94–101.

—the first steps towards a complete destruction of British institutions, which would inevitably end in the tearing-up of all property rights and the triumph of Republicanism and Revolution. The Reform agitation, recovering slowly during the later years of the Napoleonic wars, only came to command widespread support in the troublous period which followed the Peace. Thereafter it gradually gathered force until it came to a head in the decisive struggle which issued in the Reform Act of 1832.

We are concerned with this struggle here only in so far as it enters into the history of the Working-class Movement. The workers were by no means the only class which had reason to object to the unreformed Parliament. While the rich merchant or financier could find a seat in the House of Commons and climb into the governing class—this openness of the English aristocracy to the infusion of mercantile elements had been for centuries the greatest source of its strength —the growing body of industrial employers and tradesmen found itself, for the most part, excluded and unrecognised. The rapidly increasing middle-classes had no share in political power; the great towns in which they lived were grossly under-represented, or not represented at all, in the House of Commons. The tenant farmers had no share in the county franchise. And all this body of middle opinion, strongly imbued with the idea of its own growing importance, was becoming more and more critical of corruption and inefficiency in high places. The small employer who, by scraping and saving, raised himself to affluence, keenly resented the spendthrift habits of the older rich, and their little way of helping themselves, by pensions, and sinecures, out of the public purse. The sharp rise in the taxes, due

largely to war spending and the War Debt, roused a vigorous demand for economy and "business government."

At the same time, the demand for Universal Suffrage, as one of the "Rights of Man," had by no means spent the force acquired under the influence of revolutionary thought. Bentham and his followers, indeed, pooh-poohed the rights of man, and argued for Universal Suffrage on utilitarian grounds of common sense; but Major Cartwright's agitation, and the continued popularity of Paine's writings, kept the doctrine alive in its more revolutionary form. Cartwright, and still more Paine, doubtless appealed chiefly to the working class; but both Cartwright and Cobbett had also a large following among the smaller middle class, while Cobbett had, in addition, great influence with many of the farmers as well as with the labourers and artisans.

The Reform Movement from 1815 to 1832 was, indeed, essentially a popular movement in which the main body of the working class found itself in temporary alliance with the rising middle classes of the industrial towns. Naturally the latter, who had already some parliamentary influence, tended, in the main, to assume the leadership. Cobbett and Hunt, the outstanding men with influence among the workers, were both countrymen and farmers, not artisans. Gast, Lovett, Benbow, Doherty, and the other working-class leaders occupied only a secondary position. In Parliament the leader of the extreme Radicals was the millionaire Sir Francis Burdett. But none of these men really controlled the strategy of the Reform Movement. From the time when the Whig Party took up the question, the movement passed into the hands of those middle-class elements which were prepared to accept Whig leadership. Henry Brougham counted for more than Burdett in Parliament; and most of the local Reform Associations and Political Unions were mainly dominated by middle-class men of substance. Their attitude, even when it was Radical, was far more influenced by Benthamism than by the Rights of Man.

But these different groups of Reformers, however varying their real aims might be, were at least united in desiring a reform of Parliament. They tended, therefore, especially in the earlier stages of the campaign, to work together without too close a scrutiny of one another's principles. They could all demand Reform without defining too particularly what they meant. And they could all seize occasions for putting the opponents of Reform in an awkward predicament. The political importance of the famous case of Queen Caroline[1] lay largely in this, that the defence of the Queen against the King could be turned into an attack on George IV and

---

[1] The "case of Queen Caroline" refers to the divorce proceedings initiated against her by the Liverpool government in 1820. Princess Caroline of Brunswick and her husband, the Prince Regent, had been estranged for many years. Neither she nor her husband was especially noted for marital fidelity, and Caroline's reputation had been questioned publicly on several occasions. Nevertheless, she enjoyed considerable public popularity and maintained contact with the Whigs through Henry Brougham, who hoped to use her against the regent and the government. When George IV became king in 1820, she returned from residing on the Continent since 1814 to claim her rights as queen. The king sought to deny her a place as consort by having the Liverpool government institute divorce proceedings against her on grounds of adultery and scandalous behavior, but the Whigs and the crowds rallied to her defense. Their opposition forced the government to drop its action, much to the humiliation of government and king. In spite of this, however, Queen Caroline soon faded from public attention and died in 1821.—Ed.

his anti-Reform Ministers. Brougham and Denman, on the one hand, and Cobbett, on the other, were equally enthusiastic in the Queen's defence. The same bodies as passed republican resolutions one day sent "loyal addresses" to the Queen the next. Loyalty to the Queen became a form of disloyalty to the King and Constitution.

The Queen Caroline case is mentioned here because it was an important factor in giving the Reform movement a popular backing. Organised by Cobbett, a great working-class agitation sprang up in the Queen's support; and this, when the case was over, swung itself into the Reform Movement. The creation by Daniel O'Connell and his friends of the Catholic Association in Ireland (1823) was another great encouragement to the Reformers, and Irish oppression was used as a stick to beat the Government. Irishmen were active in every section of the Radical Movement in Great Britain, and especially in the working-class societies in the older towns. The struggle which led to the Catholic Emancipation Act of 1829 did a great deal to dissolve the solidity of the Tories and to prepare the way for the return of the Whig Party to power, under conditions which made parliamentary reform inevitable.

Events abroad also influenced the growth of the movement. The Spanish Revolution of 1820 and the Greek Revolution of 1821 aroused widespread sympathy, while the French and Belgian Revolutions of 1830 were among the chief causes which precipitated the crisis of 1830–1832.

In 1830 the Whigs came back to power, and their leader, Grey, at once announced that parliamentary reform would be the chief item in their policy. But what sort of reform? The Whig leaders were by temperament fully as aristocratic as the Tories, and had certainly no intention of using their power to institute a democratic system. The Reform Bill which they introduced actually went further than most people had expected, sweeping away the whole system of rotten boroughs, redistributing seats more in accordance with population, and extending the franchise to practically the whole of the middle class. But it left the manual workers almost wholly voteless, and even took away the votes they had possessed in a few boroughs having an exceptionally wide suffrage. At once the advocates of Universal Suffrage, and especially the working-class bodies which had been pressing for reform, had to decide upon their attitude to the Whig measure. Should they support it as a blow at the old order, and at least a step towards the new? Or should they oppose it as merely an attempt to substitute for the domination of the landowning aristocracy the even more hostile rule of the industrial capitalists?

In 1830 this issue was being debated in every Radical society in which the workers formed an important element. Generally, following Cobbett's lead, the main body of the workers backed the Bill, while declaring their distrust of the Whigs and reiterating their demand for a really democratic measure. But there was a left wing which denounced the Whig Bill, and refused to play any part in supporting a measure of "treason to the working class." Henry Hunt, who had been elected to Parliament in 1830 as Member for Preston, though he voted for the Bill, roundy denounced it in the House and moved many Radical amendments, which were, of course, overwhelmingly defeated.

The first Reform Bill was beaten in Committee in the House of Commons. An excited General Election followed, and gave the Reformers a big majority. A second Bill passed the Commons, only to be beaten in the House of Lords.

The excitement was by this time tremendous; and the working-class Radicals were swung into the agitation, which had clearly become a national trial of strength. Great meetings were held all over the country; the Political Unions threatened to withhold all taxes until the Bill was passed. At Bristol rioters held the city for several days, sacking the gaols, the Mansion House, and the Bishop's Palace. Derby gaol was sacked, the Nottingham Castle burnt down. In London the King was hustled, and the windows of noted anti-Reformers were broken. A third Reform Bill passed the Commons, and was thrown out by the Lords. Grey asked the King for power to create peers, and was refused. He resigned, and the Duke of Wellington tried to form a ministry, with the object of passing, against his own convictions, a Reform Bill going just far enough to divide the Reformers. The Duke failed, and Grey was recalled to power. At the close of a year of unprecedented excitement, the Lords gave way and passed the Bill. At the beginning of 1832 it received the Royal Assent and became law.

It had been impossible for the working-class bodies, in face of the opposition encountered by the Whig Bill, to press their own claim for a more far-reaching measure. They could only join in the popular cry for "the whole Bill and nothing but the Bill," and prevent it from being whittled down by further compromise with the opponents of Reform. Thus the identity of the working-class groups appeared for the time to be submerged in the general agitation.

But the struggle was, none the less, a big factor in rousing the political consciousness of the workers and preparing the way for the independent working-class political programme of the Chartists.

We can see this independent political movement beginning to develop during the years of agitation. In 1828 the London Irish had organised an Association for Civil and Political Liberty, and in 1829 this had developed into a Society for Radical Reform, supported by most of the advanced working-class Radicals in London. This in turn became, in 1830, the National Union of the Working Classes, the body which chiefly preserved left-wing Radical opinion during the critical years of the Reform struggle, and survived long enough to be the direct ancestor of working-class Chartism. In the provinces, the workers were mostly attached to the Political Unions, which were largely under middle-class leadership; but the N.U.W.C. was in close touch with the more Radical elements in these Unions, and, when the National Political Union was formed in 1831 to unite the local bodies, the working-class elements were strong enough to secure half the seats on its Council.

The Reform Act was carried chiefly by working-class agitation, and by the threat of a revolution in which the workers would have played the leading part. But it left the workers voteless and detached from them the main body of middle-class support on which they had previously relied. The middle classes obtained, in 1832, their share in political power. They had only to use their opportunities in order to ensure in the long run that their interests should dominate national policy. The vast majority of the middle class accordingly dropped out of Radical agitation, and the temporary alliance of middle and working classes was broken. . . . Attempts were made to revive it later, and in the end a new alliance was made in the Liberal-Labour compromise of the mid-Victorian period. But for the time the "betrayal" of 1832—as it was widely regarded—left the workers angry and disillusioned. They had won the battle, they felt, and yet they had none of the fruits of victory. They were left in a mood to try what they could do by their unaided efforts against a combination of the old and new ruling classes. We shall find them . . . turning to industrial action in their mood of political disillusionment. And then we shall see them, having met defeat in the industrial field, turning back to politics, there to meet with a no less crushing disaster. For the new governing class created in 1832 was far stronger, and rested on a far broader national basis, than the old. After 1832 the leading poachers turned gamekeepers. Cobbett, elected to the Reformed Parliament, found himself fighting the new power as fiercely as ever he had fought the old.

Bringing a strong interest in social and economic movements to the study of history, ASA BRIGGS (1921– .) calls attention to the variation in the support for reform throughout the country and shows the relation of the reform movement to other issues of local importance. Briggs is presently professor of history and dean of the School of Social Studies at the newly established University of Sussex. He previously held appointments at Oxford and the University of Leeds. His numerous books have touched on urban and business history as well as movements of reform, and are marked by skillful use of contemporary resources of social history. In this selection he shows the difficulty of making doctrinaire judgments on the events of 1831–1832.*

▶ ||| *A Caution Against Doctrinaire Judgments*

The Geography of Discontent

Enthusiasm for reform in the country as a whole was bound up not only with a theory of the franchise or an assertion of abstract principles but with the demand for other, sometimes even more radical, measures which had little chance of passing under an unreformed Parliament. "It must be recollected," wrote a Newcastle radical, "that a Reform in Parliament is only a MEANS to an end . . . the ENDS which that House of Commons is to accomplish are yet to be obtained." Because of the differences in social structure, economic organization and political tradition in different parts of the country, the "ends" envisaged varied—in Birmingham, Attwood and his friends pressed for currency reform; in Manchester, stress was laid on the corn laws; in old closed corporations or cathedral towns like Exeter, emphasis was placed on the need for breaking down exclusive vested interests—but everywhere the answer to the most pertinent question, "what did we want the Reform Bill FOR?" was "that it might do us some good; that it might better our situation." This, argued William Cobbett, whose *Political Register* was in the vanguard of the popular reform movement, "was what the people wanted the Reform Bill for,

* From Asa Briggs, *The Age of Improvement* (London: Longmans, Green & Co., Ltd., 1959), pp. 244–59. Reprinted by permission of Longmans, Green & Company, Ltd., and David McKay Company, Inc. Footnotes omitted.

and not for the gratification of any abstract or metaphysical whim." . . .

Although the strength of the popular radical appeal in the provinces was considerable, when Russell introduced the Whig bill there were two problems which could seldom be evaded in most places—first, the division between popular radicals and more conservative reformers, and, second, difficult relations between the Whig oligarchy and popular associations which had been set up to press for reform.

The approach to reform of economically powerful and socially established urban mercantile and manufacturing groups was substantially different from that of popular radicals. With considerable initial reluctance these groups had come round increasingly to the viewpoint that they needed direct representation in Parliament to safeguard their interests. Hitherto they had feared the effects on the smooth conduct of business of local political turmoil at election times, and had usually been content to rely on county members or representatives for neighbouring constituencies to protect their urban interests in Parliament. In the eighteenth century Burke had pointed out the lack of interest in parliamentary reform in places like Birmingham, and the first generation of industrialists, like Matthew Boulton, had certainly been unwilling to embroil themselves in election politics. With the growth of trade, however, and the increasing complexity of economic issues, the demand for separate representation of acknowledged seats of wealth, industry and commercial enterprise, gained in intensity. As a local Wolverhampton businessman put it: "Fifty years ago we were not in that need of Representatives, which we are at present, as we then manufactured nearly exclusively for home consumption, and the commercial and manufacturing districts were then identified with each other; where one flourished, both flourished. But the face of affairs is now changed—we now manufacture for the whole world, and if we have not members to promote and extend our commerce, the era of our commercial greatness is at an end." The same argument was used in Birmingham, Leeds, and Bradford; it was employed by Lord John Russell in 1820 and again in 1831; it influenced many moderate Tories, including the "Waverer" group who in the later history of the Reform Bill struggle attempted to prevent final deadlock. The argument was neither democratic nor popular: the *Manchester Guardian*, dismissed by its radical opponents as "the foul prostitute and dirty parasite of the worst section of the millowners," firmly maintained that the problem of reform was to "prevent those voters who belong to the class in society which is most accessible to bribes from over-laying and rendering of no avail the independent suffrages of people in a superior station."

Because of class cleavages in Manchester, which went back before Peterloo, the extremism of much working-class opinion, and the caution of many of the "respectable" middle classes, Manchester could not take the lead in the provincial struggle for the Reform Bill. Nor could the new industrial cities and towns of the West Riding, where economic and technical changes in the woollen and worsted industries were more recent than those in cotton and where there was bitter antagonism between new factory masters and operatives. There was perhaps no section of the Northern middle classes more enthusiastic in the cause of reform than the Yorkshire manufacturers roused by Edward Baines and the *Leeds Mercury*. They had chosen Henry Brougham as their candidate for the West Riding in 1830 and they went on to choose Macaulay as candidate for Leeds in the first "reformed election" of 1832, but their very enthusiasm stirred working-class opposition to "Whig" parliamentary reform and encouraged the operatives to press for a shortening of the working day and the end of "child slavery" in the mills. . . .

Birmingham and the Midlands, along with Newcastle in the North-East, were the areas of leadership in the battle for parliamentary reform, just because it was possible there to "harmonize and unite" the various "materials of discontent." In December 1829 Thomas Attwood set up in Birmingham a "Political Union of the Lower and Middle Classes of the People" to press for parliamentary reform. With the model of the Catholic Association very much in mind, Attwood was an opportunist in tactics, proclaiming himself a "Tory" in the early months of the Union and offering support to the Marquis of Blandford in his Ultra reform proposals. After the Whigs had introduced their Reform Bill he came round to their support, joining hands with all those who believed that "the present is the most eventful political crisis in the country." Although Attwood placed currency reform first in his own programme, he did not insist on all members of the union being currency reformers; the object of the union, as proclaimed at its first big meeting on 17 May 1830, was to "collect and organize the moral power of the country for the restoration of the people's rights, to conciliate the passions, the prejudices, and the interests of all, and to bring all to unite in one common bond of

union together." With this purpose in view, Attwood soon secured the support of Burdett and Cobbett, of Joseph Parkes, the Utilitarian, and of William Pare, the Owenite. It was never easy to maintain a completely united front, but in May 1831, when Grey appealed to the country, the Birmingham Union was not only strong locally but had set the pattern for the emergence of similar "political unions" in other parts of the country. By July 1830 there were more than ten of them; by December, they had been founded in places as far apart as Glasgow, Manchester, Liverpool, Sheffield, Newcastle, and Coventry; by March 1831, when Grey was pressing for a dissolution, the King warned him of the dangers of national "convulsion from the Land's End to John o' Groats." . . .

At heart, Grey was as suspicious of the organized unions as was the King. At a later phase in the struggle, he tried deliberately to curb their activities and authority, but in March 1831 he found it necessary to point out to the King first that "we did not cause the excitement about Reform. We found it in full vigour when we came into office" and second "that the excitement which now exists is directed to what, I think, is a safe and legitimate object. In the event of a dissolution, it would act in support of the King and Government." He went on to warn the King that "if a contrary direction is given to it, you will probably see associations all over the country; and when once they have felt their power, the history of the Catholic question will show the consequences that may be expected." Lord Durham added that if the King refused a dissolution, "feelings of disappointment, of almost reckless despair" would sweep the country. In other words, for all the

Whig fear of commotion, it was the existence of the political unions and of the radical forces they represented which were their strongest arguments in persuading the King to dissolve Parliament. And at the elections which followed, it was the vigour of provincial reforming opinion which permitted Grey to go ahead with a secure parliamentary majority. . . .

The conflict and disillusionment were to burst out at a later date; for the moment, however, during the elections themselves there was an irresistible wave of excitement for reform. Wherever there was a large and popular constituency, the reformer was in almost every case returned. At Liverpool, for example, General Gascoyne, who had proposed the motion which led to the defeat of the government, was defeated after having diligently represented the city for more than thirty years. Four reformers were returned for London, and of the eighty-two county members, almost all were pledged to the bill. "The county members," Greville pointed out in the middle of the results, "are tumbling about like ninepins." "Never, perhaps," wrote another contemporary when all the results were announced, "had any election worked so complete a transformation."

The Triumph of Reform

The political effects of the election became clear from 24 June onwards. It was then that Russell introduced a new Reform Bill, showing only minor modifications from the first. This time, the bill passed its second reading with a large majority of 136 votes (367 votes to 231). It lagged in committee, for delay was the only tactical instrument left to the opposition. Finally, on 22 September it was carried by 345 votes to 236

and was sent on to the House of Lords. . . .

Once the Reform Bill had passed the Commons, the urgent question then arose—"What will the Lords do with it?" The question had constitutional, political and social implications, and many popular orators warned the peers that they would be abolished along with the rotten boroughs if they defied the public will. The Birmingham Political Union decided to call upon all its members to refuse to pay taxes if the Lords refused to pass the bill. Despite such warnings and the arrival of wagon-loads of reform petitions from the various parts of the country, the Lords rejected the bill on 8 October by 199 votes to 158.

This gesture of defiance provoked an immediate and prolonged outburst of opposition in the country. London itself was the centre of organized and spontaneous demonstrations, and a new political body, the National Political Union was founded by Francis Place and his friends (including one old reformer of the 1790s, Thelwall) with some support from London skilled artisans. It would have nothing to do with the extreme radical demand for universal suffrage and annual parliaments, and there was soon a working-class breakaway from it, but it rallied London in support of the government in the constitutional crisis. Place was at the centre of the web of London radical politics at this time and he turned the Union into a reasonably efficient instrument, speaking in the name of "all reformers, of the masses— of the millions." Meanwhile in Birmingham monster meetings of the Political Union, with as many as 150,000 people estimated to be present, were urging all reformers to unite peacefully but unflinchingly to resist the activities of a "faction" of the aristocracy. A celebrated—and much criticized—letter from Lord John Russell to Attwood seemed to give official blessing to this entreaty. "It is impossible," Russell wrote, "that the whisper of a faction should prevail against the voice of a nation."

Where the organized power of the unions was weak, in cathedral towns, for instance, and in parts of London, there were many violent incidents in October and November 1831. The highly unpopular boroughmonger, the Duke of Newcastle, who had asked in 1830 why he should not do as he liked with his own property, was assaulted and his home attacked by a London mob; the windows of the Duke of Wellington's house were broken; the Duke of Cumberland was dragged from his horse on his way back from the House of Lords and rescued with difficulty by the police. The Archbishop of Canterbury and other bishops who had voted against the bill were insulted, jeered at, and hooted. There was rioting and arson at Nottingham and Derby, Worcester and Bath, and finally on 29 October the city centre at Bristol was sacked by an angry mob in the worst riots of the year. The words "liberty" and "slavery" which had frequently been on the lips of the Bristol slavery abolitionists were taken up by the crowds, and the weakness of both mayor and military left the mob free to do much as it wished.

The leaders of the Birmingham Political Union claimed that disastrous sequences of events in places like Bristol would have been avoided if there had been a well-organized local Political Union, but Grey and some of his colleagues (if not Russell) were very suspicious of the influence of the unions at this time. The prime minister agreed with the King that the establishment of unions was "far more mischievous and dangerous than any proceedings of a more avowed and violent character, palpably illegal and treasonable," particularly if they tried to set themselves up on a permanent footing. He maintained, however, that they could not be dissolved until the Reform Bill had passed. Restating the Whig assumption on which the whole Reform Bill had been based, he concluded that once the question of reform was settled, "all the sound part of the community would not only be separated from, but placed in direct opposition to associations whose permanent existence every reasonable man must feel to be incompatible with the safety of the country. Under such circumstances these Unions could not long continue to exist, and all the real influence and power of society would be united with that of the government in putting them down." When in November the Birmingham Political Union attempted to reshape its structure and arrange its members in local "sections" with a paramilitary organization, "a gradation of ranks and authority," the government issued a proclamation declaring that such an organization was unconstitutional and illegal. In consequence, Attwood and his friends chose to yield gracefully to the official decree. . . .

Russell introduced a third Reform Bill on 12 December 1831. It changed the test for borough disfranchisement and introduced several changes in the list of condemned constituencies, saving some which had hitherto been doomed to the loss of one member; it abandoned earlier and never popular proposals to reduce the total size of the House of Commons and distributed the seats, which hitherto were to have been suppressed, among a mixture of old and new boroughs; it simplified the conditions relating to the £10 suffrage; and it allowed freemen in boroughs, if resident, to retain their votes. The second reading of the new bill was carried by a majority of 162 votes (324 votes to 162) in December 1831. To all stalwart reformers the question now was, as one writer put it, not "what will the Lords do?" but "what will be done with the Lords?". . . .

While the Commons was debating the third bill in committee, Grey was wrestling with the difficult constitutional problem of the creation of additional peers. He was not happy himself about the consequences of creating peers on a large scale even if the King was willing to create them. "I wish to God," he wrote in January, "that it could be avoided! I sometimes think we should have done better to resign on our defeat in the House of Lords." When Althorp pointed out that if the bill were lost again because no peers had been created, "every one of us will be utterly and entirely ruined in character," Grey continued to waver, pronouncing the creation of peers "a measure of extreme violence" and "a certain evil dangerous as a precedent." In trying to cajole and soothe the King, he was also trying to cajole and soothe himself. After the King had made a somewhat vague promise in January 1832 to create what peers were required, although only if the need for them was "certain," Grey was pressed by some of his colleagues, including Althorp as well as Durham and Brougham, to have them created at once. He resisted, sharing the King's fears and knowing that a large number of his colleagues in the Cabinet, including the ex-Canningites Palmerston and Melbourne, felt as he did. His cautious approach proved justified when the un-

augmented House of Lords passed the second reading of the bill—"Waverer" votes were crucial—by a majority of 9 (184 votes to 175) on 13 April.[1]

Even now, the crisis was not over. It had to go through one final and exciting phase before the Whig triumph was complete. In committee, a motion proposed by the Tory, Lord Lyndhurst, that against Grey's express wishes consideration of the disfranchising clauses of the bill should be postponed until after the enfranchising clauses had been debated, was carried by 151 votes to 116 on 7 May. Grey with the backing of an almost unanimous cabinet decided to ask the King either to create at least fifty peers or to accept the resignation of his ministers. The King, who had been listening to other counsellors than his cabinet—his wife was generally blamed—had become increasingly alarmed at the "convulsion" of public opinion and the protests against hereditary authority, and accepted the government's resignation. To underline the seriousness of the new constitutional crisis, the House of Commons went on to pass a resolution imploring "His Majesty to call to his councils such persons only as will carry into effect, unimpaired in all its essential provisions, that bill for the Reform of the representation of the people which has recently passed this House."

For several days there was grave political and constitutional deadlock. The Political Unions, which had been relatively quiet earlier in the year, held mass demonstrations to "speak a tyrant faction's doom." In Birmingham, where there had never been any important rift between middle-class and working-class reformers throughout the struggle, Att-

[1] The Commons had carried the third reading by 355 to 239 on 23 March.

wood and his friends pledged themselves on the day of Lord Lyndhurst's motion to seek a more radical reform if the government's bill was modified or shelved. As the situation worsened the Union recruited many new members and dedicated itself to fighting the battle of reform through to final victory. In the words of its hymn,

> We raise the watchword, Liberty!
> We will, we will, we will be free.

In Manchester, where social divisions had hitherto handicapped joint action, a mass meeting was arranged to protest against the actions of the House of Lords. Above all, in London, which was now at the heart of the political struggle, a campaign was planned to try to make it impossible for a Tory government to take office. Old London institutions, like the Livery, appealed to the Commons to vote no supplies to a Tory government, and the Court of Common Council set up an emergency committee to meet from day to day. Francis Place, assisted by radicals of all hues, placarded the streets which the slogan, "to stop the Duke go for gold." His idea of a run on the banks was coupled with a scheme to organize a collective refusal to pay taxes. More ominously still, the leaders of the Rotunda joined hands with Place and there was talk of barricades and pikes, whilst Daniel O'Connell reminded a cheering audience at Westminster that "Charles I had been beheaded for listening to the advice of a foreign wife."

Meanwhile, the anti-reformers tried in vain to form a Tory government willing to carry an attenuated reform bill of its own. Peel, troubled by haunting memories of Catholic emancipation, and rightly afraid of seeking to introduce a measure which would make a mockery of his earlier resistance to all projects of extensive reform, refused to take office. Wellington, conscious only of his "duty" to his sovereign and of the danger of creating additional peers, did his best to find a team of ministers willing to act, but the political task was too much for him, quite apart from the problems created by the pressure of outside opinion. On 14 May, Wellington's spokesman in the House of Commons, Alexander Baring, was compelled to announce that the commission given to the Duke to form a ministry was "entirely at an end."

The King, who had by now lost all his popularity in the country, was left with no alternative but to ask for Grey again. Impotently angry at the way events had worked out, he kept Grey and Brougham standing when they went for their interview, but he was obliged to give them the vital note granting them permission to have enough new peers created to secure the passing of the Reform Bill. The King's secretary, Sir Herbert Taylor, who had played an important part behind the scenes throughout the whole story of the bill, followed up this granting of royal permission by sending a circular note to the bishops, the moderates, and the most active leaders of the Tory opposition in the House of Lords reminding them that it would not be necessary to create new peers at all if the Tory peers dropped their opposition. Although a handful of peers continued to protest strongly against the bill and accused Grey of acting in an "unconstitutional" manner, the bill went through its committee stage in six days, and was read for a third time on 4 June, 106 peers voting for it and only 22 against. It received the royal assent on 7 June. . . .

Some historians have made much of

the "correctness" of Tory prophecies in 1831 and 1832, and have gone so far as to claim that on the "high historic and philosophical plane, the tory case against reform was irrefutable." Such an assessment is highly debatable. Quite apart from the fanciful fears of the new shape of politics, many of which were not realized in the near future and some of which have never been realized, the Tories were themselves in a sense responsible for the dimensions of change in the Reform Bill of 1832. The gravity of the political situation in 1831 and 1832 arose from "the fault of those who had delayed Reform so long that it was necessary to do in one bill and at one time what ought to have been done long before in twenty bills, spread over more than a century." It is unprofitable in history to pursue such "moral" judgements too far and dangerous to try to dole out "high historic and philosophical" praise and blame. The Whigs themselves were always prone to do it, weaving together a tapestry of "Whig interpretation," and recently they have been criticized far more sharply than the Tories by modern historians. In fact, however, without the specific Whig contribution to the "settlement" of this question in 1832, the course of nineteenth-century English history might have been very different. By making it possible for an unreformed House of Commons to reform itself, the Whigs were successful under the leadership of a highly traditionalist peer in relieving the danger of revolution and in attaching to the Constitution "the middle classes who form the real and efficient mass of public opinion, and without whom the power of the gentry is nothing." It is impossible to say what would have been the fate of traditional British institutions if the political system had not been adapted in 1832 to fit the needs of some of the most active members of a new economy and a new society. Only in such circumstances might all the fears of the Tories have been realized. Certainly the Whigs in 1832 did a good deal to prevent the extreme radical vision of the future from becoming a reality: they made sure—to use their own language—that the "age of improvement" would not be suddenly transformed into an age of "disruption."

One of the most distinguished historians of nineteenth-century England was a Frenchman, ÉLIE HALÉVY (1870–1937), professor at the Ecole Libre des Sciences Politiques in Paris. His multivolume, and unfortunately incomplete, *History of the English People in the Nineteenth Century*, is a standard work for all students of the period, although some of his conclusions have been challenged in recent years. The first portion of the following selection is drawn from one volume of that work* and the second is from a short study on English reactions to French revolutions in the nineteenth century.† The question of how England avoided the revolutions that France experienced runs through Halévy's work on England. He is unusually conscious of the influence of the French revolution on England in 1830. However, many other historians, such as Trevelyan and Marriott, share his view.

▶ ||| *Catalyst of Reform in England*

In 1829 King Charles X had placed in office a Government of ultra-conservative ministers with the Prince de Polignac as prime minister. When the Deputies refused his cabinet their confidence he dissolved the Chamber. The new elections were held in July 1830 and in spite of ministerial pressure the Opposition increased its strength by fifty votes. Thereupon Charles issued four decrees dissolving the new Chamber before it met, restricting the franchise and abolishing the freedom of the press. In Paris the party of the tricolour replied by a rebellion whose issue was still uncertain when in England the borough elections began on July 30. But when the first county elections were held on August 5 Charles X had fled and Louis Philippe was lieutenant-general of the kingdom. Two days later he was king of the French.

The news of these events provoked in England a bewildering storm of popular feeling, which swept the country and was most unfavourable to the Gov-

---

* Pages 34–37 are taken from Élie Halévy, *History of the English People in the Nineteenth Century*, vol. 3, *The Triumph of Reform*, trans. by E. I. Watkin (London: Ernest Benn, Ltd., 1950), pp. 3–9. Reprinted by permission of Ernest Benn, Ltd., and Barnes & Noble, Inc., with footnotes omitted.

† Pages 37–39 are taken from Élie Halévy, "English Public Opinion and the French Revolutions of the Nineteenth Century," in Alfred Coville and Harold Temperley (eds.), *Studies in Anglo-French History during the Eighteenth, Nineteenth and Twentieth Centuries* (Cambridge: Cambridge University Press, 1935), pp. 51–54.

ernment. A legend sprang up and was widely believed to the effect that Wellington was Polignac's accomplice in his *coup d'état*. His brother, Lord Cowley, was ambassador at Vienna, his brother-in-law Sir Charles Bagot minister at the Hague. Was it so incredible that he maintained through these channels close communications with that alliance of monarchs which for the past decade had placed the absolutists in power in Spain, in Portugal, and finally in France? Moreover, Polignac had been the French ambassador in London when Charles X had made him prime minister. Wellington's frequent guest and intimate friend, he had no doubt returned to France encouraged by his good wishes and primed with his advice. What if the *coup d'état* he had tried to carry through in Paris should prove the prelude to a similar *coup d'état* which Wellington, a former soldier, would attempt at some future date in London? Indeed, was not the hasty dissolution of Parliament itself an attempt to override the will of the people? Fortunately Polignac's failure and Charles' fall had frustrated the plot and the new Parliament would certainly not prove so amenable as the Parliament of 1826.

To be sure the existing franchise and the disintegration of both the traditional parties did not permit of a regular battle between two groups of candidates each furnished with a programme identical throughout the entire kingdom. The Opposition was composed of very disparate groups, containing as it did Radicals, orthodox Liberals, aristocratic Whigs, Canningites, and ultra-Tories, and during the past months the Whigs had by no means shewn uncompromising hostility to Wellington. Such indeed was the confusion, which prevailed during the contest, that the ministerialists could

even claim to have increased their strength. But reliable calculations showed that, if they had gained twenty seats, they had lost fifty, a loss of about thirty seats. Moreover, the composition of their majority, if indeed they still possessed one, requires examination. The Government secured a powerful majority in Ireland, where the disappearance of the forty-shilling freeholders had rendered the influence of the great landlords preponderant, every seat in Scotland, where the elections were a farce, and a considerable number of English pocket boroughs. But it was significant that of the 236 members returned by constituencies where the franchise was more or less open only 79 were supporters of the Government, 16 were neutral, 141 belonged to the Opposition. Further what were the subjects which filled the candidates' addresses? Until the closing days of July the abolition of slavery and the necessity of retrenchment. But as soon as the revolution broke out in Paris the constitutional question took precedence over every other. To be sure the attack was not as in France directed against the person of the sovereign. George IV was dead and the new king popular; he was considered with or without justification as a friend of reform. It was the privileges of the aristocracy which were the object of attack, the excessive influence it was in a position to exercise over an unduly restricted electorate. In every constituency where the elections were more than a form the candidates found themselves obliged to promise more or less explicitly a reform of the franchise.

The Radicals were triumphant. In their view the July Revolution was the renewal of 1789; they saw France and the whole of Europe in her train following the example of the United States of America and advancing towards a system of unqualified democracy. In London and Birmingham they displayed once more, as in 1819, the tricolour flag, organized mass meetings of sympathy with the Parisian rebels, and opened subscriptions for the victims of July. Their representative in Paris was Doctor Bowring, translator of the Marseillaise, who boasted that he was the first Englishman to be granted an audience by the new king Louis Philippe, and three still very young and raw Radicals, John Mill, John Roebuck, and John Austin undertook a joint pilgrimage to Paris, were applauded in the theatre and officially received by La Fayette.

It was with more mixed feelings that the Whig aristocracy, the middle class, and in general the moderate elements of the nation, learnt the news from Paris. Who could tell during the summer and autumn months whether the French were not preparing to repeat 1792 after 1789 and give the signal for a class war in France to be followed by a crusade throughout Europe? Indeed, in August the news of the revolution at Paris produced a panic on the Stock Exchange. But on the whole public opinion was unfavourable to the Bourbons. For *The Times*, a non-party organ, Charles X from the moment of his flight was plain Charles Capet, who had no claim to anything beyond the hospitality of Great Britain. The Liberals continued to cherish the hope that Louis Philippe's experiment would prove successful, and the July Revolution be a revolution at once liberal and conservative, would in fact revive not 1789 or 1792 but 1688 and thus be a French tribute to the political wisdom of the English....

The movement now reached England itself. In Kent at harvest time some farmers attempted to replace English labour by Irish, the latter being extremely cheap. The English farm-hands expelled the Irish by force. When the time came to thresh the corn the farmers attempted to reduce their wages bill by the use of machinery. The labourers broke the machines. The disturbances spread to Sussex, Hampshire, and Wiltshire. The agitation then turned northward into Berkshire and Oxfordshire, and from there reached the eastern counties, Buckinghamshire, Huntingdon, and Northamptonshire. Sixteen counties in all were affected. The farm labourers intimidated the Irish immigrants, broke the agricultural machinery, and burned the mills. An imaginary "Captain Swing" played the part which "Captain Ludd" had played in the north twenty years earlier and terrorized the countryside. Bands of labourers traversed the country districts spreading alarm by their violent language and behaviour. They attacked the overseers of the Poor Law, whom they charged with excessive harshness in enforcing the regulations. They denounced the farmers and obtained by threats an increase in their wages of 2s. or more a day. In some instances they declared themselves the farmers' allies and espoused their cause against the Anglican clergymen. When the latter came to receive their tithe they offered violence and compelled them to abandon a third or even a half of their due. This was the first open display of anticlericalism witnessed in rural England.

Economic causes alone cannot account for this sudden outbreak; no new economic factor came into play just at this moment to render the position of the agricultural labourer in the southern counties more insupportable than it had been for months, indeed for years, previously. The factor which turned the scale was the example of France. Two years earlier the peasants of Picardy and the district around Boulogne had burned the mills. After the July revolution it seemed natural to the Kentish labourers to imitate their French comrades. It was after a tour undertaken by Cobbett, the Radical orator, that the disturbances broke out in Kent, Sussex, and Hampshire. The manifestoes circulated through the country-side copied the stereotyped formulas of French Jacobinism, and the common people were exhorted to remember Brussels and Paris. When the Government decided to take severe measures it was often found that the suspects were not agricultural labourers but smiths, joiners, artisans of every trade whom political passion not poverty had turned into agitators. The Tories maintained that this rustic rebellion had been the work of French agents. These assertions of Lord Eldon and Lord Falmouth were unsupported by a shred of evidence. But if France did not affect England by direct propaganda, she did so by the contagion of her example.

The riots were of a very mild description. The agricultural labourers confined themselves to looting, and if occasionally they employed personal violence against some particularly unpopular landlord, they were content with knocking him about. If a country house here and there were attacked, a few young men armed with fowling-pieces were sufficient to subdue the mob. And the disorders were after all confined to particular areas. The manufacturing districts of the north and north-west, which had now recovered from the crisis of 1825 and were once more enjoying a period of prosperity, were entirely unaffected. But it happened that the dis-

tricts over which the disorders occurred were those in the immediate neighbourhood of the capital. The citizen of London, seeing himself surrounded by a circle of riots, could hardly avoid the impression that rural England as a whole was in a state of anarchy. He demanded a remedy which the Tory Government decided that it was not in a position to provide. The economists ascribed the demoralization of the working class in the southern counties to the lax administration of the Poor Law in those areas. Should the Poor Law then be rendered more stringent? The Cabinet felt itself already too unpopular to incur the further unpopularity of such a measure, and in any case the medicine would require time to produce its effects. Were they to call out the troops, imprison and hang the rioters? The least step in this direction and Wellington would be accused of attempting the role of a British Polignac and might well find that instead of repressing riot he had provoked revolution. He prepared to resign.

* * *

The political history of Europe in the course of the nineteenth century may be considered as a series of insurrections against the order established by the Congress of Vienna in 1815. This order meant, in internal politics, the return, in so far as the thing was practicable, to absolutism of the type which had prevailed in Europe before 1789: in questions concerning the distribution of territories among nations it also meant the return to the *status quo ante bellum,* except for a certain number of modifications which appeared necessary, and against many of which, in fact, Western Liberalism often protested: the annexation of Genoa to Piedmont, of the Rhineland and part of Saxony to Prussia, of Belgium to Holland and of Norway to Sweden. The Mediterranean revolutions of 1820 (Spain, Portugal and Naples) were the first upheaval. They deeply impressed English opinion, and prepared the way for a new school of foreign and commercial policy under Canning and Huskisson. They did not, however, influence French politics, except that this tended at first to strengthen rather than weaken the forces of the Right. They do not, therefore, belong to my subject.

Not so the revolutions of 1830. They began in Paris, where in three days the legitimate monarchy of Charles X was overturned, and Louis-Philippe, Duke of Orleans, was made "King of the French" in his place. Then, just as in 1820 the insurrection in Spain had spread to Portugal and Italy, the insurrection in Paris spread to Switzerland, Hesse, Hamburg, Saxony, Brunswick, Belgium; and from Belgium it spread to England, where it brought about the passing of the Reform Bill.

I know that this is not the way in which the story of the passing of the Reform Bill is usually told in England. It is presented as the natural outcome of an indigenous agitation in favour of a more or less radical reform of Parliament, which began as early as the eighteenth century, was nipped in the bud by the wars with revolutionary France which followed, sprang into existence once more as soon as peace was restored, and lastly, after years of active propaganda, produced the Reform Bill. Now, it is true that the "radical" agitation was intense in the years which followed the return of peace, more particularly during the years 1817 and 1819; and that round about 1820

everybody considered that the existing electoral regime was doomed. But it was then that Lord Liverpool rallied to a more liberal conception of Toryism, with the result that when, in 1828, an economic crisis broke out which was more serious than the crises of 1816 and 1819, there was no radical agitation, and no demand for electoral reform: the country was obviously satisfied with Canning's and Huskisson's moderately liberal Toryism. Again, it is quite true that, after the passing of the Catholic Emancipation Bill in 1829, the question of Parliamentary Reform was revived. But it was a complicated and confused agitation, not to be compared with the far more serious agitation which had convulsed the country ten years earlier. It was started by Tories (the Marquis of Blandford and Attwood of Birmingham), who complained that Catholic Emancipation had been forced by a minority upon an unwilling majority, and hoped that a more democratically elected Parliament might be inspired by more genuine Tory feelings. The result was that the Liberal press expressly disowned all sympathy with the movement. When the general election began, at the end of July 1830, as a result of the death of King George IV, the only question which raised any enthusiasm was the abolition of slavery: the country as a whole was apathetic; never before had a smaller number of seats been contested.

Then came the insurrection in Paris, and the change in England was dramatically sudden. The insurrection was too popular for anyone, even Wellington, to dream of supporting an expedition by the Allies to restore the fallen monarchy; there was hardly one insignificant Tory paper to speak of him, when he came to seek a refuge in England, with the slightest touch of sympathy. But, in spite of the fact that Wellington himself had at bottom little sympathy with Charles X's and Polignac's dreams of territorial aggrandisement towards the Rhine and the Mediterranean, he was considered by everybody and could not but consider himself as *solidaire* with Charles X; and the fall of Wellington was the natural outcome of the fall of the last of the Kings of France. After which came the Reform Bill: it was not the bill drawn up by Lord Durham upon a purely French model, it was, in its final form, something different, in one respect more timid (there was no ballot), but in all respects far more bold. Does anybody quite realize today that Louis-Philippe's France, with thirty million inhabitants, only had a quarter of a million electors, while the United Kingdom of Lord Grey and Lord Melbourne, with twenty-five million inhabitants only, had about eight hundred thousand electors? And the fact remains that there would probably have been no Reform Bill in the years immediately following the death of George IV, that there would at all events have been no measure to be compared for its boldness with Lord Grey's bill, if it had not been for the French Revolution of July. Such was, at that time, the international solidarity of parties. We have here a most interesting example—and one which is quite exceptional in the history of England, of an important historical event being the direct repercussion of an event in continental, and more particularly French, history.

In a study based on careful chronology and examination of contested elections in 1830, NORMAN GASH (1912–   ) disputes Halévy's interpretation of the July Revolution in France as a catalyst in English reform. Gash finds that events in Paris aroused sympathetic interest in England, but he believes most Englishmen thought France was following an English example rather than the reverse. Gash is professor of history at St. Salvator's College, St. Andrews University, Scotland, and his detailed research of the sort shown here has exposed much of the practical workings of early nineteenth-century politics. He is the author of *Politics in the Age of Peel* and is presently working on a biography of Sir Robert Peel, the first volume of which has appeared.*

Halévy's Interpretation Disputed

The view that the English general election of 1830 was strongly and sympathetically affected by the July revolution in France is one that has never been seriously challenged even though it has not always been wholeheartedly accepted. One of the most authoritative exponents of this opinion was Halévy. In his *History of the English People* he stated that the news of the events in France, coming when the borough elections had just started and the county elections were about to begin, "provoked in England an indescribable storm of popular feeling which swept the country and was most unfavourable to the government." But Halévy was basing himself on much contemporary assertion. One of the tory contentions in the Reform Bill debates was that Grey's ministry had only come into power because of the artificial excitement caused by the French revolution. The strongly conservative *Annual Register* in its review of the year argued that as a result of the events in France "the general election took place in a period of greater public excitation, directed towards great changes in the frame of the government, than had occurred since the period of the French Revolution," and added that in no popular election did any candidate find himself a gainer by announcing himself as

* From Norman Gash, "English Reform and French Revolution in the General Election of 1830," in Richard Pares and A. J. P. Taylor (eds.), *Essays Presented to Sir Lewis Namier* (London: Macmillan & Co., Ltd., 1956), pp. 258-64, 266-71, 273-74, 287-88. Footnotes omitted.

an adherent of the Government. Wellington himself attributed to that excitement the major responsibility for his parliamentary defeat in November 1830. "The administration was beaten by two events," he wrote at the end of December. "First, the Roman Catholic question; next, the French Revolution." But though he admitted that over Catholic Emancipation "we estranged our own party," he thought the ministry would still have been too strong for the whigs, "if the French Revolution had not occurred at the very moment of the dissolution of Parliament."

In war the duke had rarely had occasion to supply explanations for defeat. Politics, as he had been finding out, was a different matter. In both, however, the retrospective accounts of beaten commanders are less valuable than their utterances during the actual campaign. Wellington, before his parliamentary defeat, showed no awareness that the general election had made it impossible for his ministry to continue. At the beginning of September he told Vesey Fitzgerald that what the government lacked was not numbers in the House of Commons but talent in the cabinet. In October he wrote to the duke of Northumberland, then lord lieutenant of Ireland, that though men's minds were unsettled on a variety of political questions, he hoped the meeting of parliament would tend to tranquillize them and that the government would get through its difficulties. In this mood of mild optimism he was not peculiar. To few people did the result of the general election seem at the time to clarify what was admittedly a confused political situation. If the ultra-tory *Standard* announced that the result would be the formation of a strong "country" party, the whig *Morning*

Chronicle talked with confidence of the overthrow of the squirearchy at the recent elections. On two points only was there general agreement: that the government had been neither influential nor popular; and that there would be a strong movement for enquiry, retrenchment and reform in the new session. Party men in government and Opposition made the conventional claims to have gained on balance from the elections. But nice statistics of this kind were almost irrelevant. Neither before nor after the election did the government command a majority in the House of Commons. Even when Wellington was writing to Fitzgerald, the Treasury whips were calculating that less than a half of the House could be reckoned as firm supporters. This, of course, did not necessarily spell doom to the ministry. The House was not based on a rigid two-party system and the organized body of the Opposition numbered less than two hundred. In these circumstances, though the position of the government was not easy, there was at least room for manoeuvre. The question posed by the 1830 election was not whether the government had lost outright control of the House of Commons, but whether the character and temper of the new House would deprive the government of its ability to manoeuvre successfully any longer.

It was privately admitted by the ministerialists during the autumn that they could not hope to stay in office without a reinforcement of "speaking talent" in the Commons. But, when it came to the point, no reinforcement was available except on condition of parliamentary reform. It was true that when the ministers abruptly resigned in November 1830, it was on another issue; but they did so to evade the question of reform and to put responsibility for that subject on their successors. Whatever Grey's personal feelings were on taking office, parliamentary reform was an inescapable legacy left to him by the outgoing government. The subject on which men soon began to differ, however, was whether this irresistible demand for reform was simply the culmination of a long domestic agitation, or the fortuitous result of a coincidence during the summer of an English general election with a French revolution.

The chronological coincidence was, in fact, rather finer than is generally realized. On 28 July *The Times* reported the promulgation of the Polignac ordinances. On 2 August came the news of rioting in Paris and republican successes; and on 3 August the English newspapers were able to give detailed accounts of the fighting and announce the formation of the provisional Government. By that date, most of the English elections were already over. In many constituencies electoral activity had started in early July and by the middle of the month candidates were taking the field all over the country. By 29 July the first elections had started and by 3 August *The Times* could report the results in over sixty constituencies and the return of over 120 members. The difference between the timing of the county and borough elections was not quite so uniform or distinct as Halévy suggested; but in general the elections in the uncontested English boroughs were decided in the last two days of July and the first two days of August; the counties and most of the contested boroughs in the first week or ten days of August.[1]

Yet how many elections were ac-

tually contested in 1830? Even in the twenty years after the Reform Act the average number of constituencies contested at a general election was only just over half. Before the Reform Act the proportion was undoubtedly smaller, even though exact statistics are hard to obtain. H. S. Smith, in his *Contested Elections* (1842), records only sixty-one contests in England and Wales at the general election of 1830. As he ignored the fifty-six rotten boroughs disfranchised in 1832 the real figure is slightly higher. But of those omitted constituencies only eight were contested in 1830, and only one of them (Stockbridge, Hants) made its return after 2 August. Even allowing for the omissions and possible defects in Smith's compilation, it is probable that little more than a quarter of the 269 English and Welsh constituencies were contested in 1830. It is true that uncontested elections frequently concealed a decision of some sort, and might even reflect a measure of public opinion. But it would necessarily be a decision taken some days, perhaps weeks, earlier and not likely therefore to be influenced by sudden extraneous events at the time of the election itself. But even with the contested elections, the real consideration is whether they were decided after the news of the successful July revolution had reached the English public through their morning newspapers on 3 August. The official *Return of Members of Parliament* (1878) gives just over a hundred English and Welsh constituencies with the date of the election return in 1830 as 3 August or later. These were not all contested, though they naturally contained a higher proportion of contests than the earlier elections. Of the sixty-one contests listed by Smith, twenty-six were already decided by 2

---

[1] In Scotland and Ireland the majority of the elections took place in the second and third weeks of August.

August. His figures must, as already indicated, be scaled up slightly. But as all but one of the contested boroughs he omitted to consider concluded their elections before 3 August, the revised total is only thirty-six. Exact figures are impossible until the whole election is subjected to large-scale research. Yet the tentative conclusion must be that probably less than forty contested constituencies in England and Wales were decided after 2 August. If so, the amount of voting open to the direct impact of the July revolution was considerably restricted.

It would be wrong, of course, to take into account merely the actual votes cast after that critical date. Atmosphere and emotion are important in politics though they are not easily translatable into statistics. Even candidates certain of their seat might be infected by popular enthusiasms or impressed by strong views among their constituents at the time of their election. Of the intense interest roused by the news from France there can be no doubt. It started not merely with the Paris riots or the Polignac ordinances but with the elections to the new French Chamber early in July. At the beginning of the month there were press comments on the probable course of the elections in France and on 9 July *The Times* had a leader on the political problems facing Charles X. French internal politics continued to occupy a large share of the foreign news and between 20 and 23 July *The Times* devoted its chief leading article almost daily to the French situation. Once the revolution broke out, both the national and the provincial press gave extremely full reports; and up to the end of August, *The Times* at least continued to make a feature of French news. Indeed, while providing its readers with a steady

flow of report and comment on affairs in France, the newspaper curiously omitted to give any general review of the results of the general election in England.

The issue, however, is not whether the British reading public took a marked interest in the revolutionary proceedings in France at this date, but whether they were prepared to draw analogies between the contemporary situation in the two countries or to derive inspiration from abroad for a forward movement at home. Some undoubtedly were; and it is perhaps symptomatic that the most important of these were drawn from the extreme wings of English politics—the ultra-radicals and the ultra-tories.

As early as the middle of July, Burdett was already using the coincidence of Liberal successes in the French elections with the start of a new and popular reign in England to urge all reformers to unite in exploiting circumstances so favourable to a reform movement. With the outbreak of the revolution in Paris, the French analogy became a feature of lower-class Radical propaganda. Hume, appearing for the first time as prospective member for Middlesex in an unopposed election, told the crowd on nomination day (5 August) that if they needed an example, a glorious one might be found in a neighbouring state; and though he had too high an opinion of his country to think that the occasion would ever arrive for such proceedings as had lately taken place in France, he hoped the people of England would be as sensible of their rights as the people of France. Cobbett in his *Political Register* contended that the effect of the French revolution must be to hasten reform in England, and in a series of speeches and lectures in the late summer and autumn proceeded to ram home the point with his usual vigorous and repetitive technique. On 16 August he presided at a dinner of Radical reformers at the London Tavern and delivered an address of congratulation to the people of Paris which was subsequently reprinted at that stronghold of Radicalism, Birmingham. Between 9 September and 7 October he delivered a set of eleven lectures on "The French and Belgian Revolutions and English Boroughmongering" at the Rotunda in Blackfriars Road. But two factors limited the effect of Cobbett's arguments. The acceptance of the July revolution as a direct political inspiration was a doctrine preached mainly to the proletarian Radicals. It is true that the whig *Morning Chronicle*, pursuing its own line of parliamentary reform, admitted in a leader of 7 August that there was much in Cobbett's view. But this was exceptional. The people in whose minds his arguments found readiest approval were for the most part the poorer, unenfranchised classes who at most could only have an indirect influence on the elections. In the second place, his propaganda developed its main strength after and not during the elections. This was perhaps inevitable. If the July revolution presented a lesson to the British public, it was one that required at least a few days for absorption. In fact, it was not until the elections were largely over that the Radical spokesmen began generally to elaborate the analogy of French revolution and English reform. From their point of view it would have been better had the events in Paris preceded rather than accompanied the English elections. The coincidence was a little too exact. . . .

It was left to the ultra-tories, from their superior station in the political world, to make more timely use of the French revolution. Not only were they themselves in a state of profound discontent with their own government, but the anticlerical character of the July revolution was in their eyes an immediate recommendation for an event which in a more normal state of mind they might have regarded very differently. Obsessed as they were by the dangers of Catholicism, they ignored the aberration of political principle involved in their support for revolution. Nevertheless their tactics were shallow and patently opportunist, and it is questionable whether they were approved by more than a minority even among the general conservative elements in the country. Their propaganda scarcely convinced themselves; it did not convince many others. In essence their campaign was a continuation of the vendetta against Wellington and Peel that had started the previous year with the Government's decision to grant Catholic Emancipation. From that date Wellington in particular had become the target for ultra-tory abuse. Indeed, on the eve of the general election it was remarked that if the Government was not outstandingly popular, it was not strongly opposed on matters of policy by any section in parliament except the ultra-tories. The unrelenting hostility of that group was characteristically shown at the end of July when the *Standard* greeted the news of the Polignac ordinances with the ironic enquiry whether things were any better in England, and whether, if the French legislature was in as bad a state as the English, there would be much loss in its dissolution. With the outbreak of the revolution in Paris, however, the *Standard* recovered from this false start, went over to the popular side, and tried instead to damage Wellington's position by identifying him with the party of reaction in France. In the worst journalistic style it first, on 2 August, hinted at Wellington's complicity with Polignac, and then, the following day, demanded that Wellington should publicly deny the charge or else resign. A few days later Sir Richard Vyvyan, one of the more unbalanced of the ultra-tory country members, took up the running. At the Cornish county election meeting at Bodmin on 6 August, he delivered a rambling and, at times, almost unintelligible speech, in the course of which he compared Peel's metropolitan police with the French gendarmerie and Wellington with James II. The purpose of his oratory, however, was clear enough. He called on all parties to join in an "anti-Wellington party"; he argued that Catholic Emancipation was not an isolated question but part of a general struggle in Europe between Liberalism and representative government on the one side, tyranny and despotism on the other; and he spoke of the evident connexion between Wellington's actions and the ordinances of Polignac. The *Standard* immediately exploited this new ally, and for the rest of August and into September continued to insinuate that the prime minister had been an accomplice of the fallen and discredited French Government.

The fact remained, however, that scarcely a person of consequence was found to believe the charge. From the outset *The Times* championed the government on this issue and dismissed the story as the invention of a stupid and malignant faction. The *Morning Chronicle*, the chief Liberal organ, also defended Wellington, though in more lukewarm fashion, against this particular calumny. An excess of generosity was not to be expected from political opponents, but the whig Liberal party as a body preferred to leave the Polignac legend as the monopoly of the *Standard* and the rest of the ultra-tory press.... Whatever Wellington's faults were as a politician, no sensible person could have thought him an accomplice to the reactionary policy of the French Government. The British public of all classes and opinions condemned the French king and his ministers, and approved the July revolution; they had little reason to believe that their own Government did not share those sentiments.

United as Englishmen were in welcoming the revolution, however, they were not necessarily conscious of any need to extract from the scenes enacted in France a lesson for their own political behaviour. Indeed, the comments passed in the press and in public speeches on the French revolution are more characteristic of a mature and stable political society than of a country ripe for rebellion. The analogy that presented itself most strongly to the ordinary English mind was between 1830 and 1688. What England had achieved a century and a half ago, France was now after a long interval endeavouring to emulate.... The analogy between 1830 and 1688, which rapidly became a stock theme in the national press, was echoed in the counties. The *Leeds Mercury*, one of the most influential of the provincial newspapers, used the comparison to refute the agitation of the ultra-radicals. To admire the French revolution and call for a similar change in England, it observed, was to show a profundity of ignorance. "Why, we had *our* "Glorious Revolution" a hundred and forty years ago." France was only copying our example and imitating our institutions. Why should Englishmen play the monkey trick of "mimicking those who are imitating us?"

Englishmen of moderate views (and in 1830 they probably constituted the bulk of the electorate) were prepared to admit defects in their constitution and wished to have them reformed; but they could not see that there was any essential similarity between the political situation in France and in England. Even in the charitable efforts made to relieve the victims of the fighting in Paris, the same attitude was apparent. Meetings were held in many parts of the country for the joint purpose of congratulating the French and raising subscriptions to assist those who had suffered in the struggle. But it was a general movement and not confined to the Radicals; and speeches made on such occasions struck the same note of robust, humanitarian and slightly complacent approval.

It would be fallacious, moreover, to assume that the profound interest created in England by the news from France was accompanied by an equally profound interest in the result of the general election; or that the people most interested in the one were also most concerned with the other. General elections under the unreformed system, with its eccentric representation and limited franchise, were of a more specialized nature than they became later in the century. The 1830 election, in the contemporary confusion of issues and parties, was not calculated to arouse particular national excitement. For the professional politicians the case was different; but it is possible that for the public at large the elections were obscured rather than illuminated by the sensational events on the Continent. *The Times,* on 4 August, discussing the tremendous public interest in the news of the July

revolution, remarked "indeed, it far exceeds even that for the home elections, in the mass of the people, those being excepted of course from its influence who are personally engaged in the latter." A week later the *Morning Chronicle* took the same view.

The paramount interest and importance of the triumphant progress of freedom in France has, in some measure, diverted public attention from scenes at home which otherwise could not have failed to arrest it. But we must not suffer ourselves to lose sight of the elating prospect which so many of the late Elections have opened to the friends of liberty in this country. . . .

In the end, of course, what counted was not what the newspapers said but how electors and candidates behaved. If the question is, how far the general election was influenced by the July revolution and how far that influence worked against the Government and in favour of reform, the answer must ultimately be sought in the elections themselves. And until the 1830 general election is analysed constituency by constituency, that answer cannot be complete. Yet the electoral realities of even a few constituencies will at least throw some light on the question. Three have been selected for enquiry. All were large constituencies; all were contested; and all decided their elections after 2 August. If the influence of the French revolution was an appreciable factor in 1830, it is presumably in this kind of constituency that it would show most clearly. . . .

[Here the author undertakes a detailed discussion of the 1830 election in a metropolitan constituency (Southwark), in a medium-size borough (Reading), and in England's largest county (Yorkshire).—Ed.]

Evidence from a limited number of elections is necessarily of itself limited. But incomplete as it is, it must at least cast some doubt on much of the generalized comment on the 1830 election that has passed into print. Seen in detail, the most striking feature of these individual elections is the importance of local and personal factors, and of domestic issues, rather than any signs of external stimulus. Government was weak but it is not true that opposition to Government was the only passport to electoral favour; and there was perhaps more respect for Wellington and Peel than has been commonly thought. Traditional party divisions existed but there were no clear party policies, and candidates came to terms as best they could with the electorate. The scene is at once more complicated and more human than the artificially simplified version offered later by observers after the event. In most constituencies the elections probably followed a familiar pattern, and if the news of the revolution brought an additional excitement, it was of a vague and diffused kind. What could not be doubted was that many electors wanted reform of some sort or another—parliamentary reform, economy, abolition of slavery, cheap bread—and that irrespective of party many candidates expressed a greater or less degree of willingness to support those objects in the House of Commons. Brougham and Burdett were probably right in saying that the new parliament would inevitably see great changes; and in that case it was clear that Wellington's minority Government, if it could not direct those changes, was bound to give way to another. But in the elections themselves, even those relatively few contested after 2 August, it is difficult to discern that the news of the French revolution was more than an accidental and superficial feature. Certainly there is little indication that the electors consciously thought of themselves as following in the footsteps of the Paris revolutionaries. The English public was immensely interested in the July revolution, but its attitude resembled less the deference of an admiring disciple than the more characteristic posture of John Bull giving comfortable and mildly patronizing approval to the belated efforts of a less fortunate neighbour. What coloured in retrospect the circumstances in which the general election of 1830 was fought, was the fact that it was followed by a disturbed autumn, the resignation of Wellington's government early in the new session, and its replacement by a new Ministry courageous enough to bring forward a measure of parliamentary reform that is still a landmark in British political history. But that, in the summer of 1830, was hidden in the future; and it was left to another general election to win the battle of reform.

J. SALWYN SCHAPIRO (1879–   ), professor
emeritus of The College of the City of New York, is
author of *Modern and Contemporary European
History* and *World in Crisis*, and has long been
interested in the history of liberalism in eighteenth- and
nineteenth-century Europe. In *Liberalism and the
Challenge of Fascism*, published shortly after the
defeat of Fascism and Nazism in World War II,
he explores the differences between the development
of liberalism in England and France and the
persistence of social forces that threatened it from
1815 to 1870. Like the Whig historians, he sees a long
tradition of liberal development in England which
developed into twentieth-century democracy and "in
England gave the cohesion and strength that comes
from national unity." Here he argues that the
transition of 1832 was effected by a compromise to
which the aristocracy were led by middle-class
Philosophical Radicals.*

▶ ‖‖ *A Compromise of Aristocracy
and Radicals*

England is the classic land of modern
liberalism. There is its original home;
there it grew steadily and flourished
mightily; there it inspired almost every
phase of life and thought; there it has
been consistently applied from age to
age, from class to class, from problem to
problem. It has been said, perhaps by
Bertrand Russell, that all Englishmen
are liberals: the Conservatives are liberals on the right, and the Laborites are
liberals on the left. That is the plain
truth. Politics, which divides these parties, is far less important than the ideal
of liberalism that unites them. An ar-

dent devotion to individual freedom and
an unbounded faith in popular government are the attitude of both parties
toward life and toward life's problems. . . .

If one wishes a year to mark the birth
of the liberal state, that year is 1688.
The Revolution of 1688 is known in
English history as the "Glorious Revolution" because it was accomplished without bloodshed—at least, without the
shedding of English blood. Considerable Irish and Scotch blood was indeed
shed before the Revolution was finally
over. Every revolution in history has

---

* From *Liberalism and the Challenge of Fascism* by J. Salwyn Schapiro, pp. 21–23, 28–30, 111–
114, 117, 120–122, 130–138. Copyright, 1949. McGraw-Hill Book Company. Used by permission.
Footnotes omitted.

been confronted by the problem of establishing a new, in place of the old and traditional, allegiance. To abolish the existing authority and to set up a new one has been fairly easy for a revolutionary party in power. What has been difficult, very difficult, has been to create a psychology of consent among the people, in order to produce a voluntary obedience to the new authority. Without this consent there could be no stability for the new government; it would not be considered "legitimate.". . .

The Revolution of 1688, "the most moderate and most successful of all revolutions," created something new in the history of mankind, the liberal state. It was the first political revolution of modern times that definitely repudiated absolute monarchy and firmly laid the basis of constitutional government. A new era in the history of England and in that of the world now began. By establishing the supremacy of Parliament, the Revolution of 1688 gave a representative body the unexampled position of being the supreme power in the government of the nation. . . .

Parliament was supreme, it is true, but Parliament was a pliant tool of the landed aristocrats through the system of rotten boroughs and limited suffrage. The parties of eighteenth-century England fitted almost perfectly into the aristocratic political system. The Whigs and Tories were not political parties in the present popular sense, but two congeries of aristocratic families—the Whig Bedfords, Grenvilles, Rockinghams, and Cavendishes, and the Tory Courtenays, Butes, and Cholmondeleys, united by close family ties and representing the same social class whose economic interests were those of the landed aristocracy. It was not, therefore, conflicts of interest, but a tradition—that of the Rev-

olution of 1688—that separated the Whigs and the Tories. The former accepted this tradition wholeheartedly as an ideal of freedom, which made them "liberal"; and the latter accepted it nonchalantly as a fact of long standing, which made them "conservative.". . .

The advent of the Industrial Revolution in the latter part of the eighteenth century was destined to undermine the system of aristocratic liberalism. A new, powerful class—the industrial capitalists—arose, seeking to entrench itself as the senior partner and to reduce the aristocrats to the position of junior partner in the government of England. In the struggle that was to take place between the two powerful classes, the advantage lay with the industrial capitalists. . . .

* * *

Unlike the situation in France after the Napoleonic Wars, that in England favored the peaceful triumph of bourgeois liberalism. There did not exist in England, as there did in France, two irreconcilable elements, each bent on the other's destruction. However bitter the feelings between the two Englands, liberal and tory—and they were very bitter—compromise was never precluded from the calculations of either side. The explanation must be sought not in the English national temperament, which is supposedly inclined to compromise, but in the fundamental fact that the English Revolution of the seventeenth century was intrinsically a political, not a social, revolution. As a class, the English aristocracy emerged virtually unscathed from the Puritan uprising and from the Revolution of 1688. Their lands were not confiscated, except in isolated cases. Their social, political, and economic privileges continued without serious modifications. And, most important of all, their heads rested securely on their shoulders. There had been no long processions to the block during the English Revolution, as there had been long processions to the guillotine during the French Revolution. What did take place was a new infusion of wealthy merchants into the ranks of the aristocracy. But the tenants remained tenants, as under their former lords, because the English Revolution "did not materially alter the existing laws in regard to land tenure. . . ." No sweeping abolition of feudal privileges took place, as in France during the French Revolution; neither were estates partitioned among the peasantry. . . .

Another fortunate element in the peaceful development of English liberalism was Parliament. It was then the only representative body in the world that exercised supreme power in the state. Despite the aristocratic character of its organization and membership, Parliament was truly a national institution. It was considered the nation in miniature, no matter how few the electors. Parliament had antiquity and continuity, which appealed to the conservative elements of the nation. And because of the revolutionary role that it had played in the struggles against Stuart despotism, Parliament was regarded as the one institution that embodied England's liberal traditions; hence it appealed to the liberal elements of the nation. Both political parties, the Tories and the Whigs, united in upholding the fundamentals of liberalism—parliamentary government and civil rights—which had definitely emerged from the Revolution of 1688. In 1815 England was the only nation in Europe that possessed in Parliament a peaceful mechanism for change that could end the "discord between a changing social condition and unchanging laws."

The aristocracy, however, controlled Parliament. It controlled the House of Lords, directly by the membership of the peers through the principle of heredity; and, indirectly, the House of Commons by proxy, through the rotten-borough system and the restricted suffrage. Aristocratic influences in the government were not limited to Parliament; they extended to the Established Church, to the endowed universities, and to the public services, civil and military. Both the Tories and the Whigs, who worked the parliamentary system and filled the offices, were representatives chiefly of the landed interests. Their power could not be broken without a drastic reform of Parliament that would introduce new elements in the electorate and new constituencies in the representative system. How could such changes be made against the certain opposition of an aristocracy tenacious of its privileges? To lose control of Parliament would mean opening the dikes to floods of radical legislation that would overwhelm the aristocracy as the ruling class. Was England to undergo a revolution against an aristocratic parliament as France had undergone a revolution against an absolute monarch?

It was plain that, in order to realize their aims, the English middle class must gain control of Parliament; and they must do it in a manner to avoid revolution, which might bring disaster to all the propertied elements. The French Revolution had begun as an attack on the property of the aristocrats, but confiscation followed confiscation with something like socialist objectives. This constituted a warning that was not lost on the English middle class, who were convinced that, at all costs, Parliament must be kept intact and under the control of the propertied classes, although the control must be shifted from the landed to the industrial interests.

A comprehensive program for the solution of this problem was the extraordinary accomplishment of the bourgeois liberals in England. With their philosophic roots deep in utilitarianism, they created two powerful movements —one, economic, in classical economy; and the other, political, in Philosophic Radicalism—both of which aimed to bring about a transformation of the English systems of society and government. So closely united and so harmonious were the bourgeois liberals that the membership of all three groups, utilitarians, classical economists, and Philosophic Radicals, was almost identical. Whatever was distinctive in each group was largely determined by its leading figure. In the case of utilitarianism, it was Bentham; in classical economy, Ricardo; and in Philosophic Radicalism, James Mill. . . .

"Philosophic Radicals" was not a felicitous designation of an active English political group, but it fitted the members perfectly. They were all intellectuals, deeply interested in the philosophic aspects of public questions as expounded by their master, Bentham. At the same time, they were active politicians and propagandists engaged in translating utilitarian principles into a political program of radical reform. Like the Fabian socialists of a later day, the Philosophic Radicals were not distinctively a third party, but they were definitely a political group with a comprehensive program of reform far in advance of anything advocated by the two major parties; and, again like the Fabians, they sought to influence public opinion, in order to bring pressure to bear on the two parties to adopt their policies. The great historic importance of English radicalism lies in the fact that it presented alternative methods to those of the French Revolution for the objectives of abolishing an old social order and inaugurating a new one. . . .

The Philosophic Radicals realized very clearly that a new balance of classes was arising in England as a result of the Industrial Revolution. A new urban population was growing rapidly, among whom there existed no nostalgia for "merrie England," no ancient loyalties to cherish, no sentiment of devotion to their betters. In the unrepresented industrial towns and in the unenfranchised urban inhabitants they beheld the possibility of a widespread movement to strike the weapon of Parliament from the hands of the aristocrats and to place it in the hands of those who would abolish the system of organized political corruption, with its romantic façade of ancient loyalties.

The plan of parliamentary reform was worked out in great detail by Bentham in his *Constitutional Code* and *Plan of Parliamentary Reform*. What Bentham demanded was a radical reform of the political system that would include the supremacy of the Commons, popular suffrage, and administrative centralization. In 1818 resolutions based on the political views of Bentham and of Mill were introduced in the House of Commons by the Benthamite, Sir Francis Burdett. These resolutions constituted a direct frontal attack on the citadel of aristocratic power, the unreformed Parliament.

In their proposals to broaden the electorate, the Philosophic Radicals came sharply up against the issue of universal suffrage. Logically universal suffrage was the practical application of the supreme principle of utilitarianism, "the greatest happiness of the greatest number," according to which each individual was to count for one and no one for more than one. The equal claim of everyone to happiness involved an equal claim of everyone to the means of attaining happiness, and "everyone" meant poor as well as rich, women as well as men, and ignorant as well as learned. In the principle of number, so dear to the utilitarians, lay the logic of political democracy. Therefore Bentham, in theory at least, favored universal suffrage for both men and women....

Logic, however, was one thing and practical politics, quite another. Being in the political arena, the Philosophic Radicals were willing and ready to compromise on the suffrage issue in the interest of the middle class. "The aim should be to develop the middle class: to this can be reduced the equalitarianism of Bentham and James Mill." Manhood suffrage aroused strenuous opposition because it was then identified with revolutionary democracy, with attacks on property, and with leveling policies. It had been adopted in 1793 by the National Convention in revolutionary France, on the principle of popular sovereignty, which, it was feared, would bring a Reign of Terror in England as it had done in France.

To Englishmen generally the "liberty of the subject," or the protection of civil rights of the individual by law, was a sacred right. But voting was a political *privilege* connected with property. Being strong upholders of the rights of property, the Philosophic Radicals were opposed to manhood suffrage, which aimed to abolish property rights in voting. Once established, it might become a precedent for attacks on property in general, as well as for attacks on privileges. They feared that, under a system of manhood suffrage, the non-propertied classes would combine politically to advance their own interest, which might prove dangerous to the middle class as well as to the aristocracy. A vote was not only an expression of opinion; even more was it an exercise of power. Manhood suffrage would give the poor political power, which they would use to redress the balance in the economic sphere. According to the Philosophic Radicals, a lowered property qualification for voting was the solution of the suffrage problem. This would maintain the property basis of voting and, at the same time, make the government "popular" by extending the suffrage. Through the process of expanding the suffrage by contracting the property qualification, the principle of number would be substituted for that of privilege in the electoral system of England. This change would lead to the suppression of aristocratic rule without incurring the dangers of revolutionary democracy. Representation on the basis of number would, according to this scheme, give the controlling power to the middle class, whose numerical superiority was sure to swamp the aristocrats and their political vassals....

The Philosophic Radicals developed a system of political strategy that was shrewdly calculated to realize their plan of reform without resorting to revolution. This system aimed.

1. To create a public opinion severely critical not only of the existing political order but also of the hallowed traditions associated with the English constitution.

2. To "soften" the Tories by continuous attacks upon them and their policies in order to bend them into an attitude of compromise.

3. To create a real opposition in Parliament by converting the Whigs to the cause of reform.

4. To give full and emphatic assurance to the propertied elements in the nation that "radicalism" was not revolutionary; that, on the contrary, it was an uncompromising champion of property rights and of constitutional methods of change.

A propaganda launched by Bentham and his followers poured an unceasing stream of vitriolic criticism of England's historic institutions, methods, and traditions. Nearly all the trenchant political pens of the period were wielded by the Philosophic Radicals and their followers, their "fellow travelers," to use a now current expression. No Burke, no Blackstone appeared, to hail the glories and sing the praises of the English constitution. Bentham's voluminous political writings might be described as an elaboration of his first book, *Fragment on Government*, in which he had violently attacked the constitution. Years later, Bentham, older and more furious, lashed out in his *Constitutional Code* against the constitution, which, he declared, was "composed of the conjunct action of force, intimidation, corruption, and delusion."

James Mill was less furious, but not less critical, than was his master. His essay "Government" was a cogent and trenchant analysis of the English constitutional system, the keystone of which was, according to Mill, the control of the political life of the nation by a landed aristocracy in order to maintain its interests against those of the people. Mill's essay became the political handbook of the Philosophic Radicals, who looked to it for both guidance and inspiration. . . .

Before long an aroused public opinion began to exercise great pressure on Parliament. This pressure was reinforced by the wave of discontent among the working class during the period of depression that followed the Napoleonic Wars. The revolutionary threat from below gave point to the agitation for parliamentary reform.

Within the Tory party an element appeared that realized that time was out of joint. Public opinion, or what passed as such in aristocratic England, was not flowing placidly in its old, accustomed channel of Parliament. Something had to be done to conciliate it, lest the revolutionary spirit be wafted from France across the Channel. A reform Tory group appeared, led by the Peels, father and son; William Huskisson; and William Wilberforce, who were inclined to favor moderate social, economic, and religious reform. Largely because of their efforts, Tory England, during the Restoration period, was not dominated by a reactionary spirit, as uncompromising as that on the Continent. A number of important reforms were enacted by Parliament: the criminal law reform of 1823; the modification of the navigation and tariff laws, to promote freer trade; the repeal of the Combination Laws against the trade-unions; the repeal of the Test and Corporation Acts against the Nonconformists; and, most important of all, Catholic emancipation. The Tories were undergoing a process of "softening," in preparation for their submission in 1832.

A far more significant result of the tactics employed by the Philosophic Radicals was that the cautious and hesitating Whigs were driven to the side of the reformers. To create a real opposition to the "stern, unbending" Tories meant the restoration of the two-party system to its full vigor. Only in a vigorous opposition, committed to reform, lay the possibility of a peaceful transition to a bourgeois liberal England. The incessant agitation for reform had influenced the Whigs far more than the Tories. In the first place the Whig tradition of 1688 was revived after the danger from Revolutionary and from Napoleonic France had passed away. The Whig party began sprouting a "left wing," led by Lord John Russell and Earl Grey, which looked with favor on plans for moderate parliamentary reform. In the second place, there had long been a sizable capitalist element, the "monied men," in the Whig party, which grew in importance as a consequence of the advance of commerce and industry during the Industrial Revolution. This capitalist element, which had infiltrated aristocratic Whig ranks, lent a willing ear to plans of political reform that would give control of Parliament to their class. Finally, the Whigs were even more sensitive than were the Tories to the rising tide of discontent among the working class. As landlords and as capitalists, they had a double motive for fearing a revolutionary overturn; hence they were more easily convinced by the Philosophic Radicals that the best way to preserve the constitution was to adapt it to changing conditions by reforming Parliament. They took to heart Burke's view that a state without the means of some change was without the means of its own conservation. For these various reasons the Whigs decided to march with the Philosophic Radicals on the reform road, though keeping well to the rear.

On their side the Philosophic Radicals, realizing the necessity of keeping the Whigs in the line of march and the Tories in a "soft" condition, proclaimed their determination to uphold the existing social order. Class diplomacy, not class war, was their line of policy. Like the Fabian socialists of a later day, the Philosophic Radicals were deeply influenced by the English tradition of compromise, and they were willing to collaborate with anyone who was willing to collaborate with them. They were quite ready to accept half a loaf, provided that it was not poisoned by too many aristocratic ingredients. Bitterly hostile to England's aristocratic regime, the Philosophic Radicals were convinced that it could gradually be dissolved by radical reforms. This method would constitute a painless revolution; it could take place, however, only when moderate conservatives joined forces with reformers. To quiet the fears of the former, it was highly essential to assure them that the policies of the Philosophic Radicals were directed toward renovation, not toward innovation. All their proposals would be consistent with constitutional methods, with a restricted suffrage, and with property rights, especially with the last. Bentham insisted that radicalism was not "dangerous" because it was strongly opposed to attacks on property rights. Such attacks, he asserted, resulted in producing more suffering among the poor than among the rich. The latter could save themselves by exporting their capital, thereby causing unemployment and destitution. Moreover, attacks on property rights, by creating a feeling of insecurity among property owners, would cause them to fear losing what was "part of our being and cannot be torn from us without rending us to the quick." Were men discouraged from acquiring property, all progress would be slowed up. If the state was obliged to take over property, such a step "should be attended with complete indemnity." Even sinecures should not be suppressed without compensation. Though strongly in favor of the abolition of slavery, Bentham's tender regard for property rights led him to oppose confiscation of property in slaves. What he favored was gradual emancipation of the slaves with compensation to their masters. . . .

The readiness of the Philosophic Radicals to agree to a propertied suffrage gave assurance to both Tories and Whigs that a reformed Parliament would not be an instrument with which to effect a revolution in property rights. To those Tories who stubbornly opposed reform, in the belief that an extension of the franchise would lead to equal division of property, Bentham replied that an equal division of property was so absurd that few held such views. "It is not *anarchy* ye are afraid of," he tartly told them, "what ye are afraid of is *good government.*"

The movement launched by the Philosophic Radicals succeeded beyond their fondest hopes. As John Stuart Mill observed in 1832, there was "nothing definite and determinate in politics except Radicalism." Its influence drew many Englishmen away from constitution worship and led them to regard favorably the changes in the governmental system advocated by the Philosophic Radicals. "The class of reasoners, called at this period Radical reformers," declared Roebuck, "had produced a much more serious effect on public opinion than superficial inquirers perceived, or interested ones would acknowledge. The important practical effect was not made evident by converging and bringing over large numbers of political partisans

from one banner or class to another, or by making them renounce one appellation and adopt another; but it was shown by affecting the conclusions of all classes, and inducing them, while they retained their old distinctive names, to reason after a new fashion and according to principles wholly different from those to which they had been previously accustomed.". . .

Discontent among the workers was spreading rapidly. They were convinced that a reformed Parliament would be an all-powerful means of bettering their social and economic condition. Hope of emancipation among the underprivileged roused them to revolutionary fervor, which had the effect of terrorizing the aristocrats and of causing apprehension among the capitalists. This situation was clearly seen by Macaulay, who, in a speech delivered in Parliament on March 2, 1831, advocated the Reform Bill on the ground that it would admit to the suffrage only those who were safe and exclude those who were unsafe. "At present," he declared, "we opposed the schemes of the revolutionists with only one half, with only one quarter of our proper force. We say, and we say justly, that it is not by mere numbers, but by property and intelligence that the nation ought to be governed. Yet, saying this, we exclude from all share in the government great masses of property and intelligence, great numbers of those who are most interested in preserving tranquility, and who know best how to preserve it. We do more. We drive over to the side of revolution those whom we shut out from power. Is this a time when the cause of law and order can spare one of its natural allies?"

Macaulay's purpose was unmistakable. It was to unite all propertied elements against the menace of a revolutionary working class, which could not be warded off by the aristocracy alone. Property was the supreme institution, "for the sake of which, chiefly, all other institutions exists." It was now threatened in its entirety; therefore, it should have as its defenders both the aristocracy and the factory owners, who were to unite against their common foe by compromising their differences regarding the reform of Parliament.

The fear of a revolutionary upheaval from below was the prime reason why the Lords yielded to the Commons in the great crisis of 1832. The provisions of the Reform Bill of 1832 were indeed moderate, and for the very reason that the threat of revolution, which had precipitated its passage, led the aristocrats to make concessions to their rivals the capitalists....

"Liberalism of the Benthamite type," declared Dicey, "was the political faith of the time. Its triumph was signalized by the Reform Act." This great measure, which marked the advent of bourgeois liberalism in England, was less a triumph of one party over another, of one class over another, of one principle over another, and more a compromise by all the parties—the Whigs, the Tories, and the Philosophic Radicals—in order to avoid a revolution. The Whigs tempered their demands. The Tories yielded. And the Philosophic Radicals accepted an extension of the suffrage so moderate that it was nothing less than a caricature of their cherished "greatest happiness" principle. It was this compromise that was the chief cause of the peaceful change from aristocratic to bourgeois liberalism. "Riot was softened into peaceable demonstration, and civil war became a party strife, waged in accordance with rules, freely admitted on either side."

Here G. D. H. COLE joins with his brother-in-law RAYMOND POSTGATE (1896–   ) to argue that reform resulted from a union of the middle class and most of the working classes behind the Whig bill as an interim measure of reform. These allies worked to convince the Whigs that failure of the bill would mean revolution, while they tried to isolate the left-wing working-class forces which insisted upon a more democratic measure than was likely to pass. The Cole-Postgate interpretation agrees with other accounts that stress Whig concession in the face of revolution, but differs from them in the importance of the role assigned to the working class. Postgate was educated at St. John's College, Oxford, and has spent several years as a journalist and civil servant. He has written extensively on labor history and Marxism, and has placed travelers in Britain in his debt by his *Good Food Guides.**

An Alliance of Middle and Working Classes

The Reform movement thus gathered force; and the economic crisis of 1825 added greatly to its strength. But the Reformers did not form at all a homogeneous group. On the right of the movement were the Whig aristocrats, desiring no more than the minimum of change that would suffice to allay middle-class discontent and to consolidate their own ascendancy. To their left were the more advanced Whigs, headed by Brougham and Durham, who held that nothing short of a clean sweep of the rotten boroughs and a new electoral system based on the middle classes would meet the needs of the time. To the left of Brougham and his *Edinburgh*

Reviewers were the Benthamites, or "Philosophic Radicals," weakly represented in Parliament, where Hume was their principal spokesman, but with a very powerful following among merchants and manufacturers and in the professional classes. The Benthamites, following their master's conversion, were by this time advocates of Manhood Suffrage; but most of them regarded so sweeping a change as practically out of the question, and were prepared to join forces with Brougham and Durham in order to push the Whigs as far as they could be persuaded to go. The Benthamites, mainly of the middle classes, had their working-class supporters, such as

* From G. D. H. Cole and Raymond Postgate, *The British Common People, 1746–1946* (New York: University Paperbacks, 1961), pp. 246–55. Reprinted by permission of Methuen & Co., Ltd., and Barnes & Noble, Inc.

Francis Place and his Westminister Radicals; and Place and his friends were to Hume and the parliamentary Radicals what Hume was to Brougham and Brougham in his turn to Lord Grey and Lord John Russell.

To the left of Place, now grown old in the service of the movement and economically a fierce adherent of Benthamite and Ricardian doctrines, stood the main body of the working class, demanding nothing less than full Manhood Suffrage. But the workers too were divided. One group, probably the largest and including a good many farmers as well as industrial workers, looked to Cobbett for leadership. A second, especially strong among the London and West Country artisans, followed Henry Hunt. Sir Francis Burdett, long Member for Westminster and the close political associate of Francis Place, had by this time become much cooler in the cause of Reform, and had largely lost his influence; and Major Cartwright, who continued his indefatigable efforts right up to his death in 1824, never commanded a large independent following. But though Cobbett and Hunt were the outstanding leaders of working-class Radicalism, their ascendancy was by no means unquestioned. To their left stood numerous local societies of working men, often Trade Unionists and Owenites as well as Reformers, who disbelieved in the possibility of Parliament reforming itself, and dreamed of unconstitutional action, or even of armed revolt, as the means of redressing their economic grievances and re-establishing society on a new basis of equality and freedom. From about 1830, the National Union of the Working Classes—at first, not national, but a London body, with its headquarters at the famous Rotunda in the Blackfriars Road—became the rallying-point for this extreme section. It founded branches in a number of provincial towns, and these soon came into conflict with the branches of the National Political Union led by Burdett and Place. . . .

In 1830 the spirit of revolt received a fresh impetus from Europe. Revolution broke out in both France and Belgium. The French people dethroned the reactionary, Charles X, and set up the "*bourgeois* monarch," Louis Philippe, in his stead. The Belgians, united to Holland against their will by the victorious Allies after Napoleon's fall, proclaimed their national independence. There were nationalist and democratic risings in Poland, Saxony, Brunswick and Hanover. A new wave of revolutionary feeling seemed to be sweeping across Europe; and in this international upheaval the forces of Labour and Socialism played for the first time a noticeable, albeit a subordinate, part. The proletariat made its first significant appearance on the streets of European cities.

The European Revolutions, especially those in France and Belgium, had a profound influence on the situation in Great Britain. They undoubtedly affected the results of the General Election which chose the first Parliament of William IV; for the election followed hard upon the "Days of July" in Paris. The new Parliament contained a Whig majority. Lord Grey was in power.

The Reform movement in the country had been rapidly gathering momentum before the revolution in France. At the beginning of 1830 Thomas Attwood, the Birmingham banker and currency reformer, had taken the lead in forming the Birmingham Political Union; and thereafter similar Unions were rapidly formed in most of the leading towns.

In the following year, under the leadership of Place and Burdett, these bodies were linked up into a National Political Union, which was thereafter the outstanding representative of the main body of Reform opinion outside Parliament.

The Birmingham Political Union was not formed on a class basis. A large part of its membership consisted of working men, but its leaders were mainly of the middle class. It stood primarily for Radical middle-class opinion, as distinct from Whiggery, and it rallied behind it those sections of the working class which were content to seek Reform through an alliance of middle-class Radicals and workers rather than by means of a proletarian revolution. Over a large part of the country the organization of the Political Unions followed the Birmingham model. They enrolled the workers, or at any rate the better-paid artisans, as members; but they were led by members of the middle classes. But in some districts, especially in the North, the workers themselves assumed the lead, and the Political Unions were predominantly working-class societies with only a sprinkling of middle-class members. In some towns two societies were founded side by side, one by the workers and one by the middle-class Radicals, and the two bodies then worked together in more or less uneasy alliance.

Until the Whigs had produced their Reform Bill, it was not necessary for the Radical societies precisely to define their attitude. Their leaders, middle-class and working-class alike, all wanted a far more radical reform than they believed the Whig Government capable of proposing; and accordingly their combined efforts were directed to organizing a pressure of public opinion that would push the Whigs as far leftward as possible. At this stage Place was devoting his efforts principally to two things—first, to organizing the existing constituencies in order to mobilize all the more Radical elements among the electorate and to secure for the new election, which he expected confidently before long, the largest possible muster of Radical, as distinct from merely Whig, candidates; and secondly, to obtaining pledges to support, after their election, a Radical measure of reform from as many as possible of the new members. Attwood meanwhile was already urging that all the Reformers should pledge themselves to refuse payment of taxes unless a really Radical Bill were passed; and Place was prepared to give qualified support to a contingent threat of tax-refusal, provided that the pledge was so worded as not to bring those who signed it prematurely into danger with the law.

At length the Whigs produced their Bill; and the Radicals were taken aback at the success which their propaganda had achieved. They had supposed that the Whigs would advance no further than the disfranchisement of a number of rotten boroughs, and the transference of the seats to the more populous counties and the growing towns. But actually the Whigs, under Brougham's and Durham's influence, and in fear of revolution unless they could destroy the unity of the Radical front, had decided to go very much further, and to establish over the whole country a uniform electoral system, with qualifications differing only as between town and county seats, on a basis broad enough to enfranchise the entire urban middle class and the main body of farmers. The workers in the towns and the labourers and small-holders in the counties were to be left voteless. But the middle class was to be offered full partnership with the existing electorate, and there was to be a thorough redistribution of seats to make the new voting rights effective. The ballot, which had been in the forefront of the Radical programme, was refused; but apart from this the Bill went much further than any section of Radical opinion had believed it possible for the Whigs to be impelled.

As soon as the terms of the Bill were known, it became indispensable for the various Radical groups to define their attitude towards it. There appeared at once wide differences among them. A large body of middle-class opinion, even among those who had joined hitherto in the demand for Manhood Suffrage, the Ballot and the rest of the traditional Radical programme, were satisfied with the Bill as it stood, and well content to desert their allies in return for the offer of membership of the governing class. The Benthamites, or Philosophic Radicals, for whom Manhood Suffrage had been an article of faith, did not take up this attitude; but they too were quite content, if they could secure as large an instalment of their full programme as the Bill offered, to postpone the rest to the indefinite future. They were not, however, by any means confident that what the Whigs promised the Whigs would or could perform. They were certain that the Parliament elected in 1830, in which there was no real Reform majority, would never pass the Bill; and they very much doubted whether the Whigs would face the necessities of a struggle which would involve new elections, the coercion of the House of Lords, and in all probability a contest with the Crown before the issue was settled. Accordingly they were determined to maintain the Radical united front of middle classes and workers, and

to use it to keep up to the end the struggle for "the Bill, the whole Bill, and nothing but the Bill." Without abandoning their insistence on the Ballot as a necessary condition of free elections, they were prepared to postpone even the Ballot and to concentrate all their forces on securing that the Bill as it stood should become law.

The working-class groups which were associated with Place and the Political Unions shared in the main the attitude of the Benthamite Radicals, though they were naturally more disposed to keep up a vocal clamour for Manhood Suffrage, and to point out that the Whig Bill meant the sovereignty of the employing class. For though they would be left voteless, and would even lose the influence they already had in the few "open" constituencies such as Westminster, they were prepared to believe that Radical Reform must come by instalments, and that they would be able to repeat the success just gained by popular pressure in a renewed agitation for a more Radical Bill before many years had passed. They were not content; but they were ready to storm the first lines of the aristocratic defences before attempting to take the citadel.

The groups of workers who stood to the left of Place were in a more difficult dilemma. Cobbett and Hunt and countless other leaders up and down the country had been unsparing in their denunciations of Whigs and Benthamites alike, telling the workers that the Whigs and the cotton-lords would unite to betray them, and that they had nothing to hope for save from their own efforts. They no more than Place had believed that the Whig Bill would go nearly as far as it did. They had expected to find themselves free to denounce a proposed alliance of the aristocracy and the rich capitalists against the workers and the small middle class. They found themselves faced with a Bill which offered to take the entire middle class into the electorate, and accordingly threatened to leave the workers to fight their battle utterly alone. Moreover, they knew that, whatever they said, a large section among the workers would follow Place's lead in agitating for the Bill as it stood.

In this difficult situation the working-class forces divided. Cobbett, after an attempt to insist on the inclusion of the Ballot as a condition of support, rallied his followers behind the demand for the whole Bill as a first instalment of Reform, without ceasing to adjure the workers to "watch the Philosophical villains" as well as the Whigs, and to stand ready to act against a new betrayal. On the other hand the National Union of the Working Classes and a few of the Northern Reform societies cried out fiercely against a measure which proposed to hand the workers over to the mercies of the capitalist class, and sought to rally the working-class forces behind a demand for nothing less than Manhood Suffrage. Henry Hunt, who had been elected as M.P. for Preston in 1829 against the powerful Stanley interest, shared the view of the extreme left; but his Preston constituents were all for the Bill, and he found himself in the House of Commons compelled to vote with the Whigs, though he continued to speak against them. In effect, it had become plain, as soon as the Whig Bill was issued, that the choice for the Radicals lay between working for the Bill and adopting a definitely revolutionary attitude; and, faced with this choice, most of the leaders rallied to the Bill, either because they were against revolution or because they felt it to be hopeless.

The Whig Bill was carried on second reading in the House of Commons by a single vote. That meant that, even apart from the attitude of the House of Lords, there was no chance at all of carrying it through Committee without large modifications, which public opinion would certainly not be prepared to accept. The Whigs had either to give way to the Tories, now reinforced by Whig malcontents who regarded the Bill as a betrayal of the Whig aristocracy, or to face a new election—and the consent of the King was needed for a dissolution. Lord Grey, convinced that nothing less than the Bill would avert the danger of revolution, decided on the second course. With many misgivings—for he disliked the Bill—the King gave way. A second General Election was held in May 1831, and the Whigs came back to Parliament with a greatly increased majority. The Bill passed through the Commons without difficulty or substantial change. It was sent up to the House of Lords in October; and the Lords promptly threw it out.

The peril in which the Bill stood in 1831 solidified the popular forces in its support. Its working-class opponents were left in a small minority, and the main mass of working-class Reformers rallied to the Political Unions in the struggle for the Bill. When the Lords rejected it, a revolution backed by the middle-class as well as the working-class Reformers seemed fully possible. All the Reform bodies clamoured for a creation of peers sufficient to ensure its passage. The Whigs had to go on, or face revolution. But they hesitated to ask the King to swamp the House of Lords by making new peers; for he might well refuse, and then revolution would be unavoidable. Grey introduced his Bill with minor changes, again passed it through the Commons, and sent it back to the Lords who, in April 1832, carried the second reading by a majority of nine votes.

But the House of Lords had not yet done with the Bill. Driven to accept the inevitability of some sort of Reform, the Lords set to work to amend the Whig measure. Grey thereupon resigned. Then followed the political crisis known as the "Days of May." Wellington, who hated all Reform, tried to form a Tory Ministry to carry through a Bill just sufficient to prevent revolution. But Peel and most of the Tories in the House of Commons refused to follow him. Grey came back to office with a pledge from the King to create, if need arose, enough new peers to ensure the passage of the Bill. But the threat was now enough. The House of Lords gave way, and the Reform Bill of 1832 became law.

This, however, is only the parliamentary side of the story. The issue was really decided in the weeks of turmoil which followed the Lords' rejection of the Bill in October 1831. For in those weeks it became manifest not only to the Whigs but to many Tories as well, and to almost the whole class of merchants and financiers, that nothing less than the Bill would now avail to prevent revolution. The Bristol Riots, in the course of which the workers had command of the city for several days, the burning of Nottingham Castle, the sack of Derby jail, and the appearance of angry crowds in the streets of London, where the King's carriage was molested, gave the governing classes warning of the temper of the people. The middle-class Reformers, though they were ready enough to use these demonstrations of force as arguments for the Bill, were in no mind to see their hopes of a *bourgeois* Parliament drowned in a Red Revolution; and they rallied all their forces behind the Whigs to secure the passage of the Bill. The Political Unions were amply supplied with money for propaganda; and they used it in consolidating their hold in opposition to the forces of the extreme left. The National Union of the Working Classes and the other opponents of the Bill, who had seemed in October about to assume the leadership of the workers, found themselves again isolated. In the final crisis of May 1832, Place and not Hunt was in control of the situation, working in close alliance with the middle-class Reformers. It was he who took up again Attwood's proposal to refuse payment of taxes, and carried his famous slogan: "To stop the Duke, go for gold," proposing to the middle classes a run on the Bank of England's gold reserve as a means of preventing Wellington from forming a government. Never since 1688 had Great Britain been so near actual revolution as in 1831; never in all the troubles of the next two decades was she to come so near to it again.

D. C. MOORE (1925–　　) challenges the concession theory of the 1832 reform, calling for a closer look at the supporters of reform and the actual provisions of the bill. Although he recognizes the strength of Radical protest, he draws attention to the "country Tory" supporters of the Grey government who were rewarded by important concessions in the franchise and redistribution provisions. He supports his conclusions by close examination of electoral behavior in the constituencies in a manner similar to Gash. Moore studied at Columbia and Cambridge universities and is presently at the University of California, Los Angeles. He has been interested in the effect of the several nineteenth-century reforms on constituency politics and recently published another article extending the views expressed here (see the bibliography) .*

Ultra-Tory Vengeance

In most of nineteenth-century Europe the growth of political democracy was essentially revolutionary. It has therefore been understood in terms of the class antagonisms which are said to have caused the Continental revolutions. In Britain, on the other hand, political democracy was established by parliamentary vote, not by revolution, by deliberation among members of the established ruling classes, not by decree of popular tribunal. The British experience would therefore seem to require a separate interpretative framework. This historians have not provided. While in England Reform Acts take the place of revolution, they are fitted to the general revolutionary pattern.

The equation of reform and revolution has held the field since the early nineteenth century. It is not unreasonable. It derives from much contemporary evidence and involves well-established social theory. Obviously, reform can not be isolated from the general context of economic and social change. Obviously, too, before the cycles of reform began, many members of the industrial middle classes were deeply annoyed at the lack of correspondence between their increasing economic strength and their continuing representational weakness in Parliament. Again, the passage of each of the three major Reform Acts was attended with considerable public disorder. And still again,

---

* From D. C. Moore, "The Other Face of Reform," *Victorian Studies*, V (1961–62), pp. 7–12, 17–18, 31–34. Some footnotes omitted.

following each Act the newly enfranchised classes were the beneficiaries of considerable legislative attention. In these circumstances, historians have tended to introduce the protagonists of reform almost solely against the background of increasing industrialization; they have tended to attribute the occurrence of reform almost solely to the activities of the various industrial classes, or to men who are regarded as their advocates; they have tended to find the meaning of reform almost solely in the needs of these new classes. Considering that each successive Reform Act was passed by an unreformed Parliament this view of the total process carries its own interpretational imperative—that each Act was a concession by which the established ruling classes managed to prevent the outbreak of revolution.

Yet for several reasons, if we take the first Reform Act as an example, this concession theory is not altogether satisfactory. In the first place, it prematurely sets the stage for an urban middle-class drama. As recent studies have increasingly tended to show, the first Reform Act did not mark a clear break in English political life. Least of all did it mark the arrival of the urban middle class to political power. In the second place, it tends to assume an unwarranted modernity in early nineteenth-century electoral behavior. And finally, it tends to distort the reform calendar.

The standard chronology of the first Reform Act posits two essential penultimate events, the death of George IV and the July Revolution in Paris. The latter bears the burden of reawakening reformist sentiments which had lain dormant for many years, the former of transmitting these sentiments to Parliament. Because George's death required

that elections take place within six months it is used as the occasion when many persons, inspired by the example of Paris, entered Parliament. However, as Professor Gash has shown, many English elections were already well under way before news of the Revolution arrived. Indeed, reform emerged from its hibernation not in the summer of 1830 but a year earlier. In the summer of 1829 it appealed neither to the aristocratic Whigs nor the urban Liberals. Apart from the Radicals, its perennial advocates, reform appealed to many Ultra-Tories, or, to use a more generic term, to many members of the Country Party. It showed the extent of their hostility towards Wellington.

It is true that the demand for political reform had long been associated with the Foxite Whigs, Liberals, and Radicals. Yet in the immediate pre-reform years it was largely monopolized by the Country Party. While it may be an exaggeration to designate as a Party the heterogeneous group of active opponents to Wellington's Government in 1829 and 1830, their opposition, as well as their demands for political, fiscal, and tariff reforms, were major phenomena of these years and important factors in the elections of 1830. As will be seen, however, by the spring of 1831 the exigencies of parliamentary politics tended to induce an historical amnesia. The efforts of the administrative Tories to reconstitute a Party after their defeat the previous November were hardly compatible with the memory that numerous Tories had played major roles in defeating them. Furthermore, because the possibility of Country Party parentage could lead to expectations that the reform progeny would take after its parents by showing a tendency towards inflation or a renewal of protection, Liberals, Radicals, and many Whigs found it essential to deny this possibility outright and to claim the baby for their own. Their plea, which the administrative Tories did their best to support, was contained in two assertions: first, that reform was a Whig-Liberal-Radical monopoly, and second, that the issue of reform was fundamentally social.

Because these assertions won the day, most historians have ignored the Country Party's demands for reform, or, like Halévy have deprecated them on two grounds: that they "lacked the support of the Whig or Liberal party leaders," and that they "lacked the support of the masses." The first of these arguments is tied to the notion that the Reform Ministry was a Whig Ministry, a notion which Professor Aspinall has recently tried to correct. The other is tied to the notion that the course of history in both the long and short term is defined by popular desires. While it must be allowed that this latter notion has some pertinence today, when means for transforming such desires into law have been highly developed, when social communities are extremely fluid, and when leaders are more often made than born, to apply it to the early nineteenth century without reservation is a distinct anachronism.

Yet inevitably the concession theory presupposes that in the early nineteenth century "the support of the masses" had specific electoral effectiveness—at least in certain constituencies. Towards this end it makes a sharp distinction between close constituencies, the corrupt and nomination boroughs, and open constituencies, best exemplified by the English counties.

Granted the social assumptions of the concession theory, the further assumption that these two types of constituency

differed from each other basically is an efficient means of explaining the votes of many M.P.'s. The majority of Members for the close constituencies voted against the second Bill on its crucial second reading. Of the eighty-two English county Members only four did so. According to the concession theory this striking disagreement may be attributed, on the one hand, to the entrenched powers of the established ruling classes in the close constituencies, which prevented the free expression of public opinion, and, on the other, to the freedom of the 40s. county freeholders. To balance the bad reputation of the former constituencies historians have endowed the latter with essentially democratic attributes.

Two questions are basic: What determined the electoral behavior of English county voters in 1830 and 1831? And how did the English counties, the open constituencies *par excellence,* differ from the corrupt and nomination boroughs?

To date, these questions—particularly the former—have been accorded but little attention. Yet the poll books, a sadly neglected source for the study of English political and social history, are readily at hand and might suggest answers.

Until 1872, when the Ballot Act separated the voter's name from the vote he cast, voting in England was a public act. After each contested election one or another local political group generally published a list of the local voters, these being identified by their places of residence or of electoral qualification. The electoral choices of each voter were entered in these lists against his name.

The purpose of publishing poll books is clear. So too is their value to historians. By providing a record of electoral behavior poll books allowed the wielders of influence, or their agents, to make sure their influences were not violated. For the historian, who can never know intimately the complexities of influence, poll books measure its effectiveness inadequately.[1] Yet in spite of their inade-

---

[1] Complete accuracy in measuring the effects of influence would require that each wielder of influence and each of his dependents be identified in positive fashion. Poll books, however, merely indicate the voter's name, and address—county poll books show his village of residence, or qualification, or both, sometimes his occupation, and his votes. They do not specify the referent of his possible dependence. When used in conjunction with local guide books will help give fairly precise indications of local landownership, county poll books provide much circumstantial evidence of influence. Yet this evidence will inevitably fail to reflect the full effectiveness of influence. It will fail to reflect influence in those instances where it only affected one of an elector's two votes, where it derived from other sources than local landownership, where the individual voter did not reside in the same locale as the other men who responded to the same influence, and where the geographical units listed in the poll books were the foci of two or more separate influences. Often this use of poll books in conjunction with local guide books will help not at all with respect to the outvoters, those who lived outside the county; its value with respect to the residents of the larger towns is doubtful. Frequently, poll books do not specify the outvoters' local geographical connections; outvoters are often lumped together under a separate heading of their own. Often, too, the voters in the larger towns were by no means politically agreed. While the size of the community might tend to make the individual resident at least somewhat anonymous, it is questionable whether the frequent lack of internal agreement in the larger towns should be taken to mean that all the voters in these towns had full individual control of their votes. Since local political agreement is found most often where landownership was concentrated in the hands of a single individual it is not surprising that diversity of local political expression should be found most often in those communities, among which most of the larger towns must be included, where several interests were focused. These considerations will explain why the use of borough poll books for a study analogous to the present one could hardly be contemplated.

quacies county poll books do reflect the existence, and to some degree at least, the effectiveness, of influence. They do so in two ways: by showing the degree of electoral agreement on the village level, a level often congruent with the boundaries of an estate, and by showing the intense localism of changes of electoral sentiment. Whenever the overall polls of a county show a change from one election to another, the change is not homogeneous throughout the county. Rather, it is a sum of local changes. Within a locality changes were generally unanimous; from one locality to another such changes were often contradictory.

In circumstances where each voter is free to express his own opinions at the polls—where the modern concept of public opinion is valid—the electoral map of a large geographical constituency will normally consist of shadings from a region where one political group is dominant to another region where another group is dominant. Within these different regions a fair amount of political disagreement will usually exist. No region will be entirely white or entirely black. The differences which define them will consist of shadings of grey.

In the nineteenth century, however, the electoral maps of the English counties were very often spotted, black and white. The Northamptonshire poll book of 1831, for example, shows that all the voters in the village of Lowick polled for the anti-Bill candidates; all the voters in the village of Aldwinkle, directly adjacent to Lowick to the east, polled for the pro-Bill candidates; with two exceptions, all the voters in the village of Brigstock, directly adjacent to Lowick to the northwest, also polled for the pro-Bill candidates. Circumstances suggest that the influences of the dominant local landowners were the major factors both in creating these local communities, and in conditioning the residents' electoral behavior.

Several considerations reinforce this interpretation. Since each elector could cast two votes at each election, he could cast many possible combinations of votes at successive elections. Yet in any particular election local agreement was the general rule. It was so in spite of the utter lack of clearly defined parties, to which, had they existed, such local agreements might possibly be attributed. But such parties, as distinct from factions, simply did not exist. This is evident both from the large number of plumped votes cast for one candidate who agreed politically with another standing in the same constituency, and also from the large number of split votes between candidates of opposing political views. Even in May 1831 when all of electoral England is supposed to have been divided on the Bill, a large proportion of pro-Bill candidates stood as individuals and were supported as individuals. In Oxfordshire, the two pro-Bill candidates went out of their ways to deny all "coalition." At the polls each enjoyed a few plumped votes and a larger number of split votes with the anti-Bill candidate, although understandably, in 1831, such a-political cross-voting was less frequent than usual. In Buckinghamshire, as *The Times* of 10 May 1831 complained, some two hundred voters whom they described as "Smith votes"—the name of a local squire—plumped for one of the two pro-Bill candidates instead of polling for both. As a result of Smith's instructions to his voters, and the instructions of others similarly inclined, the county returned one pro- and one anti-Bill Member....

Thus, a distinction must be made between the return of a vast majority of pro-Bill Members to Parliament from the English counties in 1830 and 1831, and the popularity of reform among the English "masses." To a large degree the return of these Members must be attributed to the attitudes and activities of relatively small groups of men, many of them members of the aristocracy, gentry, and urban magnate class, whose composite influences were electorally decisive.

What, then, affected the attitudes of these men?

In 1826 the majority of county Members were Ministerialists because those who wielded the predominant influence in the counties were themselves Ministerialists. Between 1826 and 1831 two things occurred which profoundly affected the political orientation of county Members. In the first place, many influential Tories went into opposition. The conjunction of three issues prompted them to do so: the Government's deflationary fiscal policy, the relaxation of the Corn Laws, and Catholic emancipation. In the second place, the urban areas of the counties, which, in general, had previously played a passive political role, awoke from their lethargy.

Growing rural opposition and urban awakening were not opposed; they were allied. The Ultra-Tories, for whom Catholic emancipation was all but equivalent to treason, were especially numerous among the aristocracy and gentry. These groups, composed predominantly of rural landowners, tended to oppose all relaxations of the Corn Laws. They also tended to oppose deflation, regarding it as the main cause of the continuing depression in agriculture. Their doing so placed them in implicit alliance with many manufacturers and provincial bankers, who, like Thomas Attwood, the organizer of the Birmingham Political Union, considered deflation responsible for the urban depression of the latter 'twenties.

Among these issues Catholic emancipation was the most crucial. The last to arise, and the most heavily charged emotionally it caught up the hostilities to the Government which the others had already engendered and refocused them upon the entire political structure. Catholic emancipation was the first step towards the first Reform Act not only because, as Professor Briggs notes, it finally dissolved the coalition which Lord Liverpool had held together, but also because it made reform respectable. Numerous Radicals and certain Whigs had long complained of the grossly unrepresentative nature of Parliament. But the questionable associates of many of these men scarcely increased the popularity of reform among the oligarchical wielders of influence. It was the passage of the Catholic Relief Act, and, even more, the manner in which it was passed, which prompted many of these latter first to appraise the political structure of the kingdom and then to add their more effective voices to the cry for reform. Their doing so committed them neither to the democratic theories espoused by some Radicals nor to the liberal views of others who wished to increase the political powers of the urban middle classes. Their adoption of reform was their way of demanding that the Government remain true to the principles of which they were the major custodians. It was not a legacy of Girondists or Jacobins but of the seventeenth-century Parliamentarians, transmitted through the economical reformers of the reign of George III. . . .

A detailed analysis of the ways in which the first Reform Act effectively restored the political powers of the landed interest is beyond the scope of this paper. However, these points may be noted: the Act withdrew certain constituencies from the control of the Government; it withdrew others from the control, or significant influence, of urban leaders.

By disfranchising or reducing the representation of the smallest boroughs, those from which Wellington's power had largely derived, the Grey Ministry gained a redistribution fund of over one hundred and forty seats. Of these, they assigned sixty-four seats to new English boroughs, primarily in the industrial north. However, the social significance of the Act tends to be distorted unless these new borough seats are balanced against the political redefinition of the English counties and the assignment to them of sixty-two new seats.

Two important aspects of the elections of 1830 and 1831 were the growth and decline of reform sentiment among the aristocracy and gentry, and the emergence of urban leaders in the arena of county politics. In 1831 urban leaders played prominent parts in returning the majority of the eighty-two English county members. The basis of their doing so lay in the relative electoral weights of the urban areas of the counties. In large measure the Act destroyed these relative weights. Thus, while urban leaders retained control of the majority of the sixty-odd seats for open boroughs which existed before 1832, and gained control of the majority of the sixty-four new borough seats, rural leaders were restored to predominant control in the majority of the eighty-two pre-reform English county seats and provided with an additional sixty-two new county seats. Unless Wellington's assertion be allowed—which, after the legislation of the previous years, many peers and more squires would hardly have done—that the nomination boroughs were the true defenders of the landed interest, on balance the landed interest came out ahead.

The Grey Ministry made no secret of their intentions regarding the English counties. In introducing the first Bill, Russell declared that the counties should be isolated from the towns so that these might not "interfere with the representation of the counties." In part this isolation was achieved by means of new electoral qualifications, in part by enfranchising new boroughs.

Before 1832, urban interference in the counties was primarily the result of most urban freeholders' being qualified as county electors. As has been seen, before 1832 many counties were electorally urban. After 1832, in most counties, the rural balance was significantly increased. This was achieved in large measure by two complementary procedures. First, the urban elements in the county electorates were reduced by enacting new borough qualifications, by providing that a freehold property in a borough should not convey a county franchise if it conveyed a borough franchise, and by granting new borough status to many of the larger towns. Second, the rural elements in the county electorates were increased by enfranchising certain copyholders and leaseholders, and by accepting the Chandos clause, which extended the right to vote to tenants at will.

The rural and aristocratic nature of the counties was still further enhanced by the means adopted of increasing their overall representation in Parliament. The Ministers suggested that most of the counties be cut into two divisions, each to return two members, and that a third member be given to all but a few of the others. As far as the Ministers were concerned, such divisions, besides increasing the number of county Members, would also increase the localism of county politics. It was Althorp's boast that this localism would weaken the tendency of certain counties to return persons on the basis of their "mere popularity."

The provisions of the measure which sought to reduce the expense of county elections involved a number of technical points of electioneering practice which are too complicated to examine in the present paper. However, they too were conceived as a means of increasing the effective powers of local oligarchs.

The similarity of intent is clear between these various provisions of the Act and the earlier suggestions of the Marquis of Blandford and articles in *Blackwood's Edinburgh Magazine*. This is not to suggest that the committee which drew up the ministerial plan took their cue from the Tories. It is to suggest that the polemical arguments which conceived of reform in social terms were largely irrelevant.

This paper does not tell the whole story of the Bill. Even less does it tell the whole story of reform. It does, however, suggest aspects of these phenomena which historians have tended to ignore: that they are far too complex to be satisfactorily described within a simplified revolutionary framework. Not only did the Bill provide an enlarged number of constituencies for representatives of the urban middle classes, it also clarified the political powers of the landed classes, the aristocracy and gentry. As their own regroupment progressed these classes settled back to a half century during which their control was absolute in the majority of the remaining small boroughs, and in all English county divisions except those in which significant urban populations lacked borough representation of their own. In practical terms, the first Reform Act was far less a blow against the powers in the State of the aristocracy and gentry than it was against the powers of the Ministers.

This realization caused dismay to some Whigs, and to many Liberals and Radicals when, as early as 1835, certain traits of the child they had claimed as their own became apparent. Their dismay is not to be wondered at. They were the disillusioned victims of one of the first of the numerous propaganda wars of the nineteenth century.

Yet while these men had not gained what they sought, they had not entirely lost. To enhance the independence of members of Parliament from Ministerial control was not to transfer power away from the ruling oligarchies. Rather, it was to transfer power from Whitehall to the constituencies. There it resided during the middle years of the century un-

til the development of centralized political parties brought it back. But the transfer of power effected by the Act provided that whenever local control changed hands, or local leaders changed their attitudes, such changes would be reflected in Parliament.

In view of the use to which Ministerial power had been put in the years before 1832—to emancipate Catholics, to liberalize the Corn Laws, and in view, also, of the Radicals' subsequent impatience with Parliament, the question arises of the relationship between the Reform Act and later "bourgeois" legislation. As observers after 1832 were not slow to notice, legislation became increasingly responsive to changes of public opinion." Such changes, however, are far slower, far more cumbersome, than those initiated by the spark of an idea within a fairly intimate group of fairly intelligent men.

The fondness of the Benthamites for Wellington and Peel in 1829 and 1830 may, indeed, be extremely significant. If history followed a logical progression (which it never does), it might be argued that the first Reform Act did more to delay such measures as the repeal of the Corn Laws than it did to accelerate them.

J. R. M. BUTLER (1889–   ) chose the passing
of the Reform Bill as the subject of his first book.
It remains a standard work and has recently
been reprinted. In this selection from it he accepts
the testimony of a leading participant in the Radical
agitation of this critical period that plans for
revolutionary action had been formulated and
would have been enacted if the reform had failed
in May of 1832. His view lends support to authors of
several schools who accept the reality of the threat
of revolution in 1832. A fellow of Trinity College,
Cambridge, from 1913, Butler held the Regius Chair
of Modern History at the university from 1947 to
1954. He interrupted his long academic career to
serve in both world wars, and he sat in Parliament as
an Independent from Cambridge in 1922–1923.
He has written several books on nineteenth-century
England and was Official Historian for the British
Official Military Histories of the War of 1939–45.*

► ## The Plan for Revolution:
A Reality

It was perhaps the day of the dissolution which really settled that the Reform Bill must become law. The night of
May 14, 1832, may have decided that it
would become so without a change of
ministers. But in the eyes of the people
of the Three Kingdoms it was May 18
on which the battle was won and which
brought the country nearest to a revolution. The Cabinet were to sit at
twelve, and Ellice had summoned a
meeting at the Treasury at one; in the
hope of convincing his colleagues of the
true state of affairs Hobhouse induced
Place to write him a letter which
might be shown to others. Place was in
his glory at such a moment, and evi-

dently with great gusto put the following menaces on paper: "Lists containing
the names, addresses, &c., of persons in
every part of the country likely to be
useful have been made. The name of
every man who has at any public meeting showed himself friendly to Reform
has been registered. Addresses and proc-
lamations to the people have been
sketched, and printed copies will, if
need be, be sent to every such person
all over the kingdom—means have been
devised to placard towns and villages,
to circulate handbills, and assemble the
people. So many men of known character, *civil* and *military*, have entered
heartily into the scheme, that their

* From J. R. M. Butler, *The Passing of the Great Reform Bill* (London: Longmans, Green &
Co., Ltd., 1914), pp. 410–11, 416–23. Footnotes omitted.

names when published will produce great effect in every desirable way. If the Duke come into power now, we shall be unable longer to "hold to the laws"—break them we must, be the consequences whatever they may, we know that all must join with us, to save their property, no matter what may be their private opinions. Towns will be barricaded—new municipal arrangements will be formed by the inhabitants, and the first town which is barricaded shuts up all banks."

Such was the business-like plan of rebellion over which advanced Reformers were gloating, while the Cabinet sat in high council in Downing Street. They resolved that, in view of the failure of the first alternative suggested in their minute of Wednesday, there was no course open but to recommend a creation of peers. They reminded the King of his former promise to make forty-one, and asked for "full and indisputable security" to carry the Reform Bill. A minute to this effect was carried to St. James's in the afternoon by Lord Grey and the Chancellor; they remained some time urging their cause with the King. . . .

It is so easy to speak loosely of the country being on the verge of revolution, and such language is so apt to be used in an indefinite and metaphorical sense, that it is important, however difficult it may be, to come to some understanding of what was, and what was not, likely to happen in England in May 1832.

First, it is essential to remember that no Tory administration was ever formed; it is inaccurate to speak of the Duke "resigning office" or resigning anything except his commission to form a government. The Whig ministers never actually gave up their seals of office;

they attended, or should have attended, to their departmental work all the time. Melbourne was still Home Secretary on May 12 when the King refused to receive the address of the Council of the Birmingham Union. This is also true of the War Office; Hobhouse was there on May 12, and George Lamb said in the House of Commons, in answer to a question, "that there had been no movement of troops except under the sanction of Ministers." Secondly, as far as the Duke of Wellington was concerned, the crisis was over on the night of Monday the 14th. He took leave of the King next morning, and had no further communication with him except on the 17th, when Taylor wrote suggesting that he should make an announcement in the Lords. Of course the King's refusal to create peers on Friday might possibly have led to the Duke making another attempt to form a government, but no such negotiations were in the air. The Duke was merely a spectator at the finish.

The ground thus partly cleared, an attempt may be made to estimate the true state of things. For the Reformers' arrangements Place's account, written about five years later but interspersed with contemporary letters and documents, is the main authority. Though no safe guide as to events occurring in Downing Street or at St. James's, he was absolutely at the heart of the middle class political arrangements in the capital, and corresponded with Radicals in the great towns. Familiar with the industrial conditions of London from his youth up, he had given his life to the study of questions affecting the working people, and had been brought by his labours into close contact with many of them engaged in different trades and in different places. Only eight years before, he pulled the principal wires in the agitation against the Combination Laws. He had also become acquainted with the intellectual Radicals in and out of Parliament, such as Bentham, Hume, Burdett, Hobhouse, and Grote; his rooms at Charing Cross were the political centre of middle class London. He was the founder of the National Political Union and a member of its council. Therefore he had every means of knowing the plans he describes. He had moreover a remarkably accurate mind, very little biassed by emotion; he was much more inclined to irony than to exaggeration. Where his knowledge was not at first hand, he usually gives his authority. Hence there is every reason for accepting his evidence on matters of fact, and his conjectures were based on wider knowledge than is usual concerning popular politics.

Something has been already said of the strategy adopted. The provincial delegates were to hurry home as soon as a Tory ministry was announced; they were to be replaced at headquarters by deputies from the towns, who were to form a permanent committee of public safety. The first blow would be aimed at the nation's credit. It was hoped that the Commons would refuse supplies; in any case no taxes would be paid, and a run would be made on all banks. As to the former, it is true that the great part of the revenue did not come from direct taxation; but a general refusal on the part of the Reforming bourgeoisie would be very serious, as Melbourne admitted, and distrained goods would not be easily sold. As to the strength of the demand for gold, there is much mystery; between three and four hundred thousand pounds were said to have been withdrawn from the Bank on Monday and Tuesday, and Place said this was

"a mere demonstration"; provincial banks must assuredly have collapsed. It was hoped that this would be enough for the Duke. If not, provisional governments would barricade all the towns, beginning with Birmingham. The troops would be kept from leaving London by the threat of disturbance there. Above all the general stoppage of business would throw vast numbers of ill-organised men out of employment; however little they might know of what the Reform Bill meant, they would have a vague idea that it would bring lower prices and better wages. Place hoped that funds would be forthcoming "to feed and lead the people"; but even if they were not the excitement would be no less dangerous to the Government.

In these circumstances he did not expect there would be serious fighting with the troops; if there should be, he had no fear of the event. The days of revolution in Paris were big in men's minds during these months, and it was not held possible that Englishmen could fail where Frenchmen, and even Belgians, had succeeded. The great scheme of a mammoth meeting of several millions had been given up, but we have it on Croker's authority that some thousands of Manchester operatives had been marched up to London; on the first news of Wellington's failure they had been withdrawn and quartered in neighbouring villages, where they were supporting themselves by begging. "At the election of 1868 an old labourer in the agricultural Borough of Woodstock told a Liberal canvasser from Oxford that in his youth arms had been stored in his father's cottage so as to be in readiness for the outbreak which was to take place if Lord Grey's Reform Bill was finally defeated." To lead these irregular forces the Reformers had secured, Place tells us, "a large number of able officers." Unfortunately we have little but this meagre statement. In December General Sir G. Cockburn wrote to Grey suggesting the enrolment of a National Guard, organised by parishes, as a possible means of overawing the Lords. Parkes also mentions a few names, but it is hardly surprising that such secrets should not have been made public property. On the whole Place was convinced the commotion—he would not call it a civil war—would not last over a few days, though in that time much irreparable damage would be done.

It would be most interesting to know what part the leading Whigs would have taken—whether Durham, for instance, would have sanctioned a fighting policy, or even drawn the sword himself. The position of Hobhouse, as the late Secretary at War, would have been yet more delicate. It is most unlikely that any others of the Cabinet would have sympathised with forcible revolution; indeed they hardly realised that any such thing was contemplated. It must also be held extremely doubtful whether the Commons would have refused supplies when it came to the point. The Government majority on Ebrington's motion approving the advice to create peers fell to eighty—a decline of fifty on the corresponding vote in October—and this would have been a far stronger step, amounting in fact to defiance of the King's personal wish. The idea was favoured openly by several speakers in the House, but it would appear that a motion to this effect was beaten at Brooks's on Sunday night, the party agreeing to support the bill in any case, even if proposed by the Duke. It is practically certain that the House would not have consented to destroy the King's

Government. The people would have fought their own battle.

On the other hand most Tories seem to have made light of the thought of resistance, had the Duke accepted office. Croker was sure the Government might be carried on with the Duke at the Horse Guards, and the *Standard* believed that "a fortnight's firm government would put down the unions and the meetings without bayonet or blood," adding: "The present excitement is not so great as that which prevailed in 1810 or 1817—nothing to be compared with that which raged in 1820 about the Queen—and yet there was no difficulty found in suppressing these riots." The difference was that in the present case the excitement was organised. This conviction tallies with the universal idea of the advanced Reformers that the Duke would use force to quiet the country. There was a tradition in Attwood's family that warrants had actually been prepared for his arrest and that of other leading unionists, but that Grey on returning to power found them still unsigned. It is difficult to believe this as stated; however, the Duke's reported remark that he knew a way to keep the people quiet turned attention to the army, and any unusual incident was jealously noted. It has been said before that Hobhouse was at the War Office during the entire period, and it is hardly possible that any orders could have emanated from the Duke. The fact that Lord Fitzroy Somerset, military secretary to Lord Hill, called at Apsley House is not sufficient. He was a friend of the Duke's and had consulted him as to military arrangements with regard to the intended meeting in White Conduit Fields in November 1831. The rough-sharpening of swords by the Greys at

Birmingham can hardly be supposed, without direct evidence, to have been intended to suppress a peaceful crowd, nor was the holding of the Guards in readiness on May 14 a political move. The *Poor Man's Guardian* held Hobhouse, not Wellington, responsible for gathering of troops towards "the Wen." So any opinions that may be formed of the Duke's probable policy, had he taken office and found himself faced by an insurrection, must be pure guesses. And, as a matter of fact, at the supreme moment of popular excitement, the Duke had no intention whatever of taking office. Genuine therefore as the Reformers' preparations were, their suspicions of him were unfounded after Monday night. The revolution was most completely organised four days after the probability of its occurrence had practically disappeared. But if Manners Sutton had not delayed his acceptance, and if the formation of a Tory ministry had been announced, as Lord Carnarvon wished, on Monday, an insurrection on the plan described by Place must almost certainly have broken out.

The difficulty of conjecturing its probable issue is enhanced by the fact that most of the upper classes seem to have had no conception of what was going on beneath the surface. The aristocracy, says Place, "could not imagine that any real danger could result from the rejection of the Reform Bill, in any way to affect themselves." They apprehended nothing more serious than a common riot. Hobhouse was content to receive his information from Place. If, as seems certain, Place's descriptions are correct, it is a most memorable case of a Government utterly incapable of understanding or coping with a critical situation. The zeal of the people was a

force quite apart from, and undirected by, the leaders of the popular party in Parliament. Reformers had no doubts of their success, even if the army should remain loyal; and this they thought unlikely. When in November 1831 the Duke drew up a scheme for the defence of London in case of riot, the forces at the disposal of the War Office consisted of four regiments of cavalry in London, with a regiment and a squadron from the south near by; twelve guns, five battalions of Foot Guards, and 500 marines. It is improbable that a much greater force was available in May, though troops were said to be converging on London from the provinces. England was at the time divided into four military districts; the troops in all of them had been occupied in maintaining order at various times in the last few months, and during these very weeks Sir Henry Bouverie had his hands full in keeping the peace among the strikers in the Durham coal-field. In the whole of the Northern District, which included Cheshire and Nottingham, there were three cavalry regiments; one of these was responsible "for the whole of the Clothing district of Yorkshire, and for the Coal district on the Tyne and Wear." At Birmingham there were two troops of the Greys—about 150 effective men. There can be no doubt that the constant employment of the military in industrial disputes and ordinary disturbances must have done something to lessen the awe they inspired among working men.

As to the loyalty of the army, there were rumors that the troops in London had promised to fire high, while we have Alexander Somerville's direct testimony as to the temper of many in the ranks at Birmingham. They would quell a riot, but would not interfere for merely political reasons. The Hertfordshire Yeomanry sent in their resignations to Hatfield as soon as the fall of the Whig Government was announced. From the inability of any force, civil or military, to prevent riots at various places earlier in the history of the bill, it seems very unlikely that an organised attempt, at each great centre, to take over the control of the town could have been resisted. Most certainly 150 troopers, tinged with disaffection, could not have coerced the populace of Birmingham. In London the Duke would have been prepared "to lay open in a minute any house or church" with artillery fire, but success must have been extraordinarily difficult in the face of a population predominantly Radical and fired by the story of the French barricades, with a hostile House of Commons too sitting at Westminster, and the Bank very probably suspending payment. Had the people won, it is doubtful what would have happened. Place himself hazarded no more than the certain "establishment of a representative government in all its parts." All along the Revolution of July was the model; it was even ironically suggested that the Duke of Sussex, who had been forbidden the Court in consequence of his behaviour during the crisis, might play the part of Louis Philippe. But doubtless King William was safe enough, and it would not have been the winners of the victory who would have controlled its results.

JOSEPH HAMBURGER (1922–   ) is an assistant professor of political science at Yale University, and the book from which this selection is drawn grew out of a study of Philosophical Radicalism. Hamburger was struck by the relation between James Mill's theories of political change and the events of 1831–1832 and decided to attempt an evaluation of the reality of the much-discussed threat of revolution. He concludes that the Whigs' fear of revolution was a lever used by the Radicals to frighten the aristocracy into relinquishing a portion of their power. His interpretation offers a contrast not only to the Butler view but also to Moore's evaluation of the idea of concession. Hamburger has recently published another book, *Intellectuals in Politics: John Stuart Mill and the Philosophical Radicals.**

▶ ‖ ## The Threat of Revolution: A Radical Bluff

There are many political situations in which efforts are made to influence perceptions of the potential for violence in a society and to manipulate anxieties about revolution among one's political antagonists. These are not confined to international politics, where the use of violence is within the range of expected responses, but also are to be found in domestic politics, especially where the legitimacy of a political order is sufficiently discredited that restraints on the use of violence become seriously weakened. In such situations efforts will be made, more or less consciously, to gain political ends by attempting to influence the government's assessment of social cleavages and the possibility of open conflict. James Mill is notable for having formulated a theory of political change that provides for the use of such tactics. Indeed, since he thought of the press as the main instrument of intimidation, he may be seen as an early advocate of the tactics that look upon the press and the distribution of "news" as part of the "overall weaponry" of politics. Although the press was widely used in this way during the struggle over the Reform Bill, Mill and a small group of associates were unique for having done so self-consciously, systematically, with skill, and with a degree of success.

Statements of fact often become in-

* From Joseph Hamburger, *James Mill and the Art of Revolution,* "Yale Studies in Political Science," no. 8 (New Haven, Conn.: Yale University Press, 1963), pp. vii–viii, 21–23, 34–35, 114–16, 125–29, 252–57, 261–63. Footnotes omitted.

terwined with rhetorical purpose, opening the door to exaggeration and even
dissimulation. Even if participants are
misled, political analysis should not accept rhetorical statements as necessarily accurate descriptions. With regard to the situation in 1831–32, this
raises a question about the reality of the
threat of revolution that was said to
exist, and an attempt is made to deter-
mine the validity of such claims. . . .

Throughout this period, even though
the more nervous members of the governing classes dreaded revolution and
saw evidence of it in public meetings
and in radical journals, the leaders of
the radical movement, with France in
mind, rejected the role of conspirator or
demagogue and thought of themselves
as anything but revolutionaries.

There is no one of whom this was
more true than James Mill. His desire
for extensive reform informed all he did
and thought, whether it was his jour-
nalism or his administrative activities on
behalf of the East India Company, or
even his *History of British India*, which,
it has been argued, carried an esoteric
critique of English society. Even the education he gave to his son can be said
to have had this purpose. Yet no Tory
had a more discerning eye for and genuine horror of threats to the social order.
He was a university student at Edinburgh from 1790 to 1793, but there is
no evidence that he uttered a word of
sympathy for the French Revolution.
And while he referred to the French as
a nation that had "dared to lift its eyes
to liberty," he sharply condemned the
result "when some hired ruffians in the
metropolis were allowed to give law to
the whole nation." He expressed great
distaste for Henry Hunt, the main
speaker at the Peterloo meeting,
whom he called "a demagogue . . . that

appeals to the rabble." And his view
that the spread of Hodgskin's economic
beliefs "would be the subversion of
civilized society" does not encourage a
belief that he was irresponsible in his
radicalism. At the same time, however,
he was a republican, an agnostic, and
a democrat.

Wanting fundamental changes in the
constitution, yet above all else anxious
to avoid violence, Mill, like other radicals, turned to extra-Parliamentary politics. Here the traditional "rights" of
public meeting and petition and the
unanimous agreement that liberty of the
press was an established "principle" of
the constitution gave some scope for action. Despite the risks attending the
exercise of these rights, they gave some
foundation to the belief that public
opinion was not totally irrelevant to the
deliberations of even an unreformed
Parliament. . . .

While Mill was firmly attached to
nonviolent methods, he was in a sense
revolutionary in his political goals, for he
sought a fundamental change in the
constitution of government so that the
legislature would be genuinely and
fully representative of the people and
not dominated by a small aristocracy.
"The real object to be aimed at in the
composition of a legislature," Mill said,
"is to prevent the predominance of the
interest of any individual, or of any
class; because, if such interest predomi-
nates . . . it will be promoted at the
expense of the community." Applying
this principle to the British case, Mill
held that "in the composition of the English legislature, the predominance of the
aristocracy is so complete, that whatever
they wish to do, they always have it in
their power to do—whatever they wish
to prevent, they always have it in their
power to prevent." He therefore be-

lieved that "no change can, directly, be any improvement whatsoever in the British legislature, which does not substitute the predominance of the general interest to the existing predominance of a particular interest." . . .

Assuming the desirability of representative government, Mill turned to the question of how this fundamental change could be achieved. The difficulty, as he saw it, arose from his belief, which was fundamental to his psychological theory and at the foundation of his political speculations, that "rulers," like all persons acted to maximize, and therefore perpetuate, their power. This belief prevented Mill from conceiving even the possibility of concessions being voluntarily granted by an oligarchy. Acting from selfish motives, which were the only ones Mill would acknowledge, an oligarchy would defend its superior position with force if necessary. Since Mill wished to achieve fundamental reforms without violence, it became necessary to devise means by which an oligarchy would be led to grant concessions out of self-interest. . . .

Because of their antirevolutionary orientation, the Whigs adopted tactics complementary to Mill's, and they did so in a way that enhanced the influence of anyone following Mill's recommendations. Mill sought a fundamental change in the constitution, and he was willing to stimulate popular demand to the point at which it appeared to be revolutionary. On the other side, the Whigs above all sought to avoid revolution, and they were willing to concede a fundamental constitutional change to achieve this goal. Both were anxious to avoid violence and to facilitate peaceful change. But for the Whigs this was a primary goal, whereas for Mill it was to be made to appear secondary. Thus

the Whigs, by making their determination to avoid violence so evident, were especially vulnerable to Mill's tactics.

There were, of course, numerous arguments that moved the Whigs to support reform. . . . Now, in the face of agitation and many symptoms of unrest, the Whigs approached Parliamentary reform as a means of reducing discontents and the threat of revolution they held out. All other arguments for reform were subordinated to the Whig contention that reform was necessary in order to avoid revolution. It was not uncommon to draw analogies with 1789. Durham, one of the authors of the Reform Bill, for example, expressed the view that the French Revolution, as well as the Revolution of 1641 and the separation of the North American colonies, "might all have been averted by timely and wise concession." Had this been done, he said, "the people would have been satisfied, the ancient institutions of the country ameliorated, the altar, the throne, and the aristocracy preserved from the horrible fate which afterwards befell them.". . .

The belief that the threat of revolution was real is especially worthy of scrutiny in view of the fact that some of those who voiced the threat in 1831–32 clearly intended it as rhetoric. James Mill in outlining tactics for the achievement of fundamental constitutional changes by peaceful means had argued that concessions would be made provided the governing classes saw revolution as the only alternative to such concessions. The success of such tactics, then, depended on the image of public feelings held by those in a position to make the concessions. Concessions would be granted, Mill said, from a fear of the consequences of withholding them. The crucial thing was to stimulate fear. How it was done was less important. Of course, fear is not the result of rhetoric alone, nor did Mill assume that rhetoric alone would be sufficient. But he did not exclude the use of rhetoric in a way that would stimulate greater fear than was justified by the actual circumstances. Thus in advising the editor of the *Examiner* in 1831 Mill said the people "should appear to be ready and impatient to break out into outrage, *without actually breaking out.*" That Mill would allow misrepresentation is even more clear from his observations concerning "the rule of veracity" in political situations. While it is important, Mill says, that men be able to confide in one another and that therefore truth not be violated, "There are circumstances, however, in which another man is not entitled to the truth"; these circumstances "create a radical distinction" and "constitute a class by themselves" and are "subject to rules altogether different." . . . "In no instance is any man less entitled to right information, than when he would employ it for the perpetuation of misrule." In these circumstances wrong information is "not a breach of morality, but on the contrary a meritorious act."

Not only did Mill's doctrine allow for deliberate misrepresentation, but his associates, when looking back on the events of 1831–32, show that they at least thought of themselves as having practiced deception. There is John Arthur Roebuck writing in later years about the passing of the Reform Bill. . . . In an anonymous article published in 1848 Roebuck confessed that public feeling was often described, not as it was, but as it was meant to appear. He acknowledged the existence of genuine excitement: "Yet," he said, "to attain our end, much was said that no one really believed; much was done that no one would like to own. . . . often, when there was no danger, the cry of alarm was raised to keep the House of Lords and the aristocracy generally in what was termed a state of wholesome terror. When the Bill proceeded with ease . . . a grave calm was preserved in our demeanour and writings . . . when its provisions were threatened . . . black clouds rose obedient to our call, as regularly as on the stage at the scene-shifter's command; our language grew violent, we stormed, we threatened and prophesied, and, like some other prophets, we were determined to accomplish our own predictions. Processions, meetings, harangues, revolutionary resolutions, banners, mobs, assemblages both by night and day, all like a furious hurricane, swept over the face of the political waters." In contrast to the "noisy orators who appeared important," those "who pulled the strings in this strange puppet-show were cool-headed, *retiring,* sagacious, determined men." They "avoided publicity," but they were, as one always found in such situations, the "one or two ruling minds, to the public unknown.". . .

Public opinion was favorable to the Reform Bill. About this there can be no doubt. It was at times even an excited public that made demands for reform. But was this revolutionary excitement? Is it appropriate to interpret the events of 1831–32 in the context of the French Revolution? Was it so difficult to maintain public order that one must assume the country to have been in a revolutionary situation? For that matter, short of revolutionary excitement, one may ask whether "the public fury" of which

Halévy (among many others) spoke, was so pervasive and typical as has been represented.

At least those who made greatest use of the rhetoric of revolution did not think that it corresponded to reality. Parkes and Place—certainly well-placed observers—reveal in private correspondence with friends that they did not believe all that they said in public about the threat of revolution. Writing to Grote on October 16, 1831, just a week after the Lords' rejection of the second Bill, Place expressed concern that public opinion had "reached its crisis . . . and has passed it without producing any good effect on the ministers." The danger was that public opinion, "rapidly declining . . . may settle down among the working classes and to a great extent among the middle classes into sulkiness," and that, "the common people shall become sullen as their immediate superiors indifferent, they will concur in nothing ministers will propose, by any demonstrations publicly made." It was for this reason that he feared, not an outbreak, but moderation, and thus he chastised Grote for what he thought an overcautious speech delivered to an assembly of merchants and bankers. At this time he also told Burdett that there was a "falling off of the excitement" and that "the people are settling down into sulkiness." James Mill seems to have shared this estimate; "I am terrified, mainly," he wrote to Fonblanque, "at any collapse in the public mind." Yet, despite his concern about sullenness among the people, this was the very time when Place spoke the "language of menace" and "wholesome terror" to the Ministry. Three days before writing confidentially to Grote he had led the deputation to

Grey (described by Roebuck), to whom he expressed "apprehension that [a prorogation till after Christmas] might lead to a violent revolution, the result of which no man could predict." One of Place's colleagues, Bowyer, a Clerkenwell bookseller who was later to serve on the Council of the National Political Union, has also recorded that "much apprehension still existed [in early October] as to whether any popular movement would take place in the event of the Bill being rejected, sufficient to work upon the fears of the Court, and to retain the Ministry in office"; and he noted that after the rejection "no movement of the working people, of any important character, seemed likely to take place." But such apprehension did not prevent Place from warning Hobhouse (who had the ear of Cabinet Ministers) that impatience among the people was such that "[financial] Panic is now in an incipient state." Lord Grey, he warned, ought to make an unequivocal declaration of his determination to have the "whole Bill."

"The delay of such a declaration," Place wrote, "may put a stop in one hour to the circulation of Bank of England notes, shut up all the shops and factories and turn the whole of the working people into the streets." If this "incipient panic" were to "be developed," then "the whole Government is destroyed at once, never again to be restored in its present form." . . .

The same discrepancy between accounts of public feeling that were sent to the press or to the Ministers directly and descriptions given to intimates can be found in some of Parkes' descriptions of extra-Parliamentary activities at Birmingham. While he did not go so far as Place, he clearly indicated how serious he believed the threat of revolution to be when in October he boasted that "six of us here could order the people, as a field officer at a review puts his regiment through their exercise." Such docility among the people was hardly compatible with a genuine belief that revolution was imminent. Far from really thinking the people difficult to control, he said "it is just possible that we may be able to bring about a Revolution but it would be through the worst of the people." As for organizing resistance, Parkes confessed that "if a Tory juste milieu comes in we *shall* have a half measure," for "there is *not* sufficient virtue in even the best part of the people to resist, and to enforce their rights." To Place he complained, "I do all I can . . . considering the *mixed* state of the Public." And in April 1832, Parkes was said to have complained about "how difficult it is to keep the people together." While portraying the Birmingham leaders to the government as militant and reckless, he privately complained that he did as much as he could. "I draw the resolutions," he said, "as strong a dose as the patients would swallow, and their stomachs would retain." Yet, despite these circumstances, he had warned Althorp, with whom he conducted a highly confidential correspondence and with whom he had a secret interview, that it is "no use now shying the word Revolution: they [the Cabinet] must make one or the People *will*." . . .

The government's response to the possibility of national organization among the few radical politicians who talked of violence was a sensible precaution. But there is little evidence that any effective organization existed among Radicals. Yet if a revolutionary threat was

to take on reality, it was organization and leadership that were needed. But this sort of organization, as so many other conditions that make up a revolutionary situation, was absent. The so-called working-class unions, which were the only ones openly talking of violence, were few in number and weakly supported and, furthermore, they were divided by personal and tactical disagreement (this anticipating the split between moral and physical-force Chartism). The working-class unions were openly hostile to the political unions that supported the Reform Ministry, even though these unions were the only ones that could at least pretend to have mass support. And these unions were at most loosely connected, the connection between, Parkes in Birmingham and Place in London providing the most effective and perhaps the only link between any of them.

The lack of any effective organization among the various bodies committed to fundamental change reflected the variety of purposes among extra-Parliamentary politicians, and this was an obstacle to the establishment of that ideological unity that can give leadership and militancy to a revolutionary movement. Among the possible leaders of such a movement, some had political purposes and some economic, some particular grievances and some a broad vision of a new society. . . . It was not only variety of purpose and disagreement in principle among the radical politicians that hindered the formation of a revolutionary movement. There was also the resistance to ideological commitment among the public as well. Most reformers were moved by particular grievances and agitated on behalf of particular remedies. Thus there were, in the main, separate "movements" in connection with Catholic Emancipation, the Reform Bill, the Poor Law (that is, reaction to it), and the Corn Laws. There is some continuity in principle and in personnel, but not much. . . .

Still another consideration reduced the likelihood of revolution. The cleavages and hostilities between classes that exist in all societies can have revolutionary implications if political issues are discussed in a way that facilitates the expression of those hostilities generated by the class system. When this happens the political process draws to itself emotions that might otherwise be restrained or at least be sublimated into other spheres. But the Reform Bill struggle had the opposite effect. . . . There were very few suggestions of abolition of the House of Lords during the Reform Bill agitation; the remedy for the Lords' opposition to the Bill was the creation not the abolition of peers. It was principally the working-class unions that saw the Reform Bill as a class measure; in their view it was for the exclusive benefit of the middle class, and this is the interpretation that has found greatest appeal among historians. But the working-class radicals, even if they were correct, failed to persuade their contemporaries that the Bill ought to have been exclusively discussed in terms of its effects on social and economic classes. Indeed, class labels are not at all prominent in discussions of the Reform Bill, and the agitation for it did not become the occasion for sharpening those class cleavages that of course existed. . . .

The only recurring symptom of . . . hostility to a national institution in 1831–32 involved the Church, or at least its bishops, twenty-one of whom, of the twenty-three who voted, declared against the Reform Bill in October 1831,

providing the margin by which it was defeated (it lost by 41 votes). It was after this that the Bishop's Palace was attacked at Bristol, with Davis, the Bristol rioter, concentrating his violent abuse on the bishops. During October and November there were several occasions on which effigies of bishops were burned; at a Newcastle meeting a banner showed a figure of death, its foot trampling the mitre. Much of this hostility arose from varied sources not directly related to the Reform Bill, but which existed by virtue of the role of the Church Establishment in the context of social life and even in the economy. This hostility coalesced with political feelings, each reinforcing the other, and the result was the most impassioned expression of hostility during these years. But it was not enough to bring down the political edifice. . . .

Despite all the talk of revolution in 1831–32, there does not appear to have been much reality behind the alleged threat. Adopting this view, however, does not mean that the social structure was perfectly harmonious, or that the country was without problems and its people without discontent. There was economic distress in 1831 arising from unemployment and increased food prices. There were discontents that were made abundantly evident in the strikes in the mining areas, in the disturbances among the technologically unemployed handloom weavers, and among the farm laborers who felt threatened by the introduction of threshing machines. The disturbances attending these and other dislocations in the economy were part of the broad changes attending industrialization, and in the short run they could only reduce the stability of society. But to acknowledge this does not require that the society at any moment be

viewed as resting on crumbling founda-
tions. Yet there has been a tendency to
make just this assumption. This is exemplified in an extreme way by the
Hammonds, whose judgment of the in-
stability of the social order was strongly
influenced by the emphasis they gave
to the economic deprivation and social
disorganization that were among the
consequences of industrialization. They
visualized the working class as having
been "naturally contented" in an earlier
age, and as "naturally discontented" in
the nineteenth century. Now politicians
had to practice the "art of preserving
discipline among a vast population des-
titute of the traditions and restraints of
a settled and conservative society, dis-
satisfied with its inevitable lot and
ready for disorder and blind violence."
This view of a society which in its nature made men "ready" for disorder
gives an exaggerated significance to
whatever symptoms of disorder are
found. Various circumstances gave
credence to such a view. For example,
there was the rioting. There were many
expressions of genuine fear of revolution. And there was the prominent use
of a rhetoric that held out threats of
violent revolution. But the rioting,
which is usually mentioned to show the
presence of a revolutionary situation,
may have indicated nothing more than
an inadequate police force. Had professional police forces existed throughout
the country it is unlikely that the evidence of revolution provided by a
riotous populace would have been
available. It is worth noting that London, which had such a police force, had
the reputation for being apathetic at the
very time that other towns, without police, gave the appearance of being in-
surrectionary. With regard to the fears
of revolution felt by many persons at
the time, it should be said that such
fears were a permanent part of the early
Victorian mentality, especially among
upper-middle class, intellectually ori-
ented persons whose impressions were
likely to be recorded; in themselves
they do not verify a hypothesis concerning the existence of a revolutionary situation in 1831–32. As for those who
talked much about the imminence of
revolution, at least in some cases "much
was said that no one really believed,"
and such rhetoric was not confined to
occasional speeches at public meetings,
for it made its way to the government
and it appeared in some of the most influential newspapers as well. Yet, given
theoretical views that assume the likelihood of revolution, such rhetoric (like
the expressions of fear or the petty rioting), becomes evidence of the existence
of a revolutionary situation. Once such
theoretical dispositions are given up, the
evidence is seen in a different light.
Thus Clapham, having done just this,
said that he has "never been able to find
any moment in the nineteenth century
at which, so far as I could judge, the
risks of violent revolution, or of anything like it, were so great as to make it
necessary for historians to explain why
no violent revolution took place. . . . the
risk was never high."

Some historians in searching for the reason why England did not experience revolution in the nineteenth century when it swept over the rest of Europe have found their answer in evangelical religion, especially Methodism. Emotional religious movements distracted the attention of bourgeois and working-class people who could have become revolutionary activists, they say, and by their politically conservative outlook turned these people into supporters of the existing order. The first and best-known spokesman for this interpretation is ÉLIE HALÉVY, who presented it in 1912 in the first volume of his *History of the English People in the Nineteenth Century*. Although speaking here of England in 1815, he believes evangelical influence extended into the period beyond.*

The Restraint of Methodism

The progress of Methodism was tending to render the Protestant Dissenters political conservatives. As their interest in theological polemics had cooled, they had lost their old taste for discussion, their former love of argument. And as their prejudices in favour of ecclesiastical autonomy weakened, their individualism in politics weakened simultaneously. Intermediate between the sects in the strict sense of the word and the Established Church, Methodism filled the gap between these rival bodies. The Methodists, and especially the Wesleyan Methodists, although in fact Nonconformists, refused to regard themselves as entirely cut off from the Anglican Church. The members of the connection admitted an obligation to communicate according to the Anglican rite when unable to communicate in one of their chapels; and their ministry claimed to be not the enemy but the assistant or the locum tenens of a clergy which neglected its duties. And the other sects were infected with the same spirit. During the first fifteen years of the nineteenth century only isolated and eccentric individuals among the Nonconformists demanded either a reform of the constitution of the national Church in conformity with their ideas, or disestablishment and equal rights for all denominations.

* From Élie Halévy, *History of the English People in the Nineteenth Century*, vol. 1, *England in 1815*, trans. by E. I. Watkin and D. A. Barker (London: Ernest Benn, Ltd., 1949), pp. 423–28. Reprinted by permission of Ernest Benn, Ltd., and Barnes & Noble, Inc. Footnotes omitted.

But for all this the division was not less clearly marked than formerly between the social classes from which the Establishment and the sects respectively derived their adherents. In some respects we might even say that the line of demarcation was drawn more rigidly than ever before. From the beginning Nonconformity had been the religion of the middle class and particularly of the lower middle class. Nevertheless, in the eighteenth century Dissenters sat in the House of Lords, and on occasion boys of noble family had received their education in the seminaries conducted by Nonconformist ministers. Now both these things had become impossible. Nor was the number of wealthy Nonconformist merchants on the increase. In the normal course the more wealthy Dissenters went over to the Church of England. If a successful man of business wished to enter the governing class, to entertain at his country seat the clergy or the gentry of the neighbourhood, to obtain a title or a position in the Civil Service, he must not be a Dissenter. The wealthy Dissenter, therefore, was only too ready to yield to the entreaties of his wife, herself perhaps the daughter of an "episcopalian" family, or of his sons, who were eager to see the family enjoy a social position in keeping with its wealth and with the education they had received. He would seize the first opportunity to pick a quarrel with his pastor or with one of the influential members of the congregation. He thus escaped the moral supervision exercised by the fellow members of his congregation, and which he had so often found galling, and attended the worship of the Established Church where there was no obligation of religious zeal, and where

the squire was his fellow worshipper. Puritan nonconformity thus tended to become a transitional creed, a stage in the history of an English family. The unskilled labourer becomes in turn a skilled workman, an artisan, the head of a small business, a business man possessed of a modest capital, and as he rises out of the barbarism in which the working class was plunged, he becomes a Nonconformist. If he himself rises still higher on the social ladder, or if his children rise after his death, he or they go over to the Church of England.

Nor was there the slightest difficulty in effecting the transition from one form of religion to another. The constitution of the Wesleyan body rendered the transition imperceptible. And what is most characteristic of the new spirit in Dissent is its acceptance of this subordinate position. The middle-class Nonconformist was content to be despised by the members of a Church which his own family might some day enter. He compensated himself by indulging an even deeper contempt for the common people of the fields or factories from whom his family had emerged.

Why was it that of all the countries of Europe England has been the most free from revolutions, violent crises, and sudden changes? We have sought in vain to find the explanation by an analysis of her political institutions and economic organization. Her political institutions were such that society might easily have lapsed into anarchy had there existed in England a bourgeoisie animated by the spirit of revolution. And a system of economic production that was in fact totally without organization of any kind would have plunged the kingdom into violent revolution had the working classes found in the middle class leaders to provide it with a definite ideal, a creed, a practical programme. But the *élite* of the working class, the hard-working and capable bourgeois, had been imbued by the evangelical movement with a spirit from which the established order had nothing to fear.

No doubt the English Nonconformists continued to oppose any movement towards bureaucracy. Without freedom of association they could not exist. But for all their freedom of theological difference the sects agreed among themselves and with the national authorities to impose on the nation a rigorous ethical conformity and at least an outward respect for the Christian social order. With their passion for liberty they united a devotion to order, and in the last resort the latter predominated. Hence freedom of association proved in the end the restriction of individual freedom and the authority of custom replaced and almost superseded the authority of law. And this is modern England. On the Continent the leaders of the English labour movement are sometimes blamed for their middle-class morality and want of imagination, at others praised for their solid virtue and capacity for organization. Perhaps these qualities and defects are inseparable; in any case they derive from a common origin. The majority of the leaders of the great trade-union movement that would arise in England within a few years of 1815 will belong to the Nonconformist sects. They will often be local preachers, that is practically speaking ministers. Their spiritual ancestors were the founders of Methodism. In the vast work of social organization which is one of the dominant characteristics of nineteenth-century England, it would

be difficult to overestimate the part played by the Wesleyan revival.

We can watch between 1792 and 1815 an uninterrupted decline of the revolutionary spirit among the sects. During the first years of the war the Dissenters of rationalist and republican leanings were loud in the utterance of their beliefs. In 1792, when Price and Priestley by their imprudent declarations of republicanism had compromised the sect of which they were the luminaries, the aristocracy and the populace combined against it. Chapels were sacked, congregations dared not meet. Tory politicians and Anglican bishops were not slow to exploit the unpopularity of the democratic Dissenters to the detriment of Nonconformity as a whole. Canning in his *Anti-Jacobin Magazine* was unwearied in his denunciations. In every revolutionary he saw either a Dissenter or a former Dissenter or a friend of Dissenters. In the associations recently formed by the Independents and Baptists to organize an itinerant ministry he saw a scheme plotted by political societies to preach under the disguise of Christianity, republicanism, Deism, perhaps even Atheism. Bishop Horsley of Rochester, in a famous charge, attacked the Methodists as conscious or unconscious agents of the Atheistic and Jacobin propaganda. What, he asked, was the true character of these religious of apparently religious societies which met every evening in the towns and country villages? of these fanatical and uneducated preachers? of this federation of religious congregations at the very moment when the federation of political associations had been declared illegal? "The Jacobins of this country, I very much fear, are at this moment making a tool of Methodism just as the illuminées of Bavaria make a tool of freemasonry; while the real Methodist, like the real Freemason, is kept in utter ignorance of the wicked enterprise the counterfeit has in hand."

When, however, we investigate what actually was taking place in the Nonconformist bodies, we discover that such denunciations are not to be taken very seriously. The only congregations in which republicanism was predominant were the Presbyterian, precisely the least numerous and the least prosperous, and their Jacobinism was hastening their decline. When in 1798 a Baptist pastor, the Rev. John Martin, declared in a sermon that, "should the French land, some, yea many, of these different and differing people" [the Dissenters] "would unite to encourage the French," the entire denomination was in arms. After a hasty inquiry Martin was expelled from the sect. It is safe to say that the advocates of revolution were the exception among the Baptists and Independents. Their most eloquent pastors denounced the political creed of Jacobism. Robert Hall, Baptist preacher at Cambridge and a friend of Mackintosh, preached a famous sermon in 1800 attacking what he called Modern Infidelity. By this he understood the principles of the French Revolution. The Congregationalist preacher William Bengo Collyer made himself famous in 1804 and 1805 by his patriotic sermons to the volunteers. The subscribers to his "Lectures on the Proofs of Scripture Truth" included Lord Grenville, Robert

Southey, and three Anglican bishops. And all contemporary evidence agrees that if the old Nonconformist denominations remained faithful to Whiggism, the vast majority of their members belonged to the right wing of the party.

When the anti-Jacobins made their charges universal and attacked the Methodist preachers, the injustice became scandalous, the calumny almost self-evident; for the sect was on principle conservative. At the time of the American War, when Price, Priestley, and Wide Dissent as a body declared for the rebels, John Wesley had published two pamphlets, whose circulation extended to several thousands to inculcate loyalty in the colonists and the British public. In 1792 the statutes of the Wesleyan body expressly demanded from their members loyalty and obedience to the King and his Government. "None of us," ran their declaration, "shall either in writing or in conversation speak lightly or irreverently of the Government. We are to observe that the oracles of God command us to be subject to the higher powers; and that honour to the King is there connected with the fear of God." Such conduct ensured that in spite of the calumnies of writers and speakers among the supporters of the Government the unpopularity of Jacobin principles did not prejudice the Methodist propaganda. The new type of Nonconformity, evangelical and pietist, was gaining ground every year.

While conceding the conservative tendencies inherent in Methodist political philosophy, ROBERT F. WEARMOUTH (1882–1963) calls attention to the democratic example presented to Radical groups by Methodist organization and ideals. Many working-class political groups consciously patterned themselves after Methodist class organization and drew their leadership from religious groups. Wearmouth worked as a young boy in the coal-mine region of northeastern England, after which he served in the army in India. On completion of his army service, he entered the Primitive Methodist ministry and served in many different parts of the country. During ministries in Birmingham and London he began research into the relation between Methodism, the working class, and the trade union movement and subsequently published several volumes on the subject. On his retirement he returned to the northeast where he continued to appear in churches in the Darlington and Newcastle circuits till the end of his life.

▶ *The Dynamics of Methodism*

The Reform Bill, which was finally passed in 1832, did not satisfy the ultra Radicals among the working classes. Only the middle classes had been appeased for the moment. The former felt they had been betrayed. So they continued their fight for reform. The betrayal of the lower classes had been foreseen by some of their leaders, and a working-class political society was formed in London as early as April 2, 1831. According to William Lovett, "The National Union of Working Classes" sprang out of another society called "The British Association for promoting Co-operative Knowledge." The latter was a branch of Robert Owen's plan for establishing a new order. It was formed on May 11, 1829, principally by some people who belonged to the London Co-operative Trading Association. Those who took a prominent part in the movement were James Watson, William Lovett, John Cleave, George Foskett, Robert Whigg, Philip and George Shene, William Millard, Thomas Powell, Henry Hetherington, and Benjamin Warden, all working men. These men endeavoured to form co-operative societies on those parts of Owen's

From Robert F. Wearmouth, *Methodism and the Working-Class Movements of England, 1800–1850* (London: Epworth Press, 1947), pp. 87–88, 90–94, 223–225. Footnotes omitted.

scheme which they believed would be acceptable to the people. This was done while Owen was in America. "Many persons who were strictly religious were alarmed at some of the proceedings of the British Association, especially at many of its members attending and supporting Mr. Owen's Sunday morning lectures." A few months before the dissolution of the British Association, some carpenters named Hetherington, Warden, and Foskett met at Argyle Street on April 2, 1831, and called themselves the "Metropolitan Trades Union." The name was afterwards changed into "The National Union of Working Classes." They met for three weeks at Argyle Street, then on April 20, they moved to 36, Castle Street, Oxford Market. On May 25, a declaration and rules were brought forward by Hetherington and his two companions. The British Association having terminated its existence, some of its members joined the new society. William Benbow afterwards became a member, and the meeting place was transferred to his Coffee House at Temple Bar. . . .

The private meetings of the National Union of Working Classes were called classes. They were similar to the class meetings of the Political Protestants and Union Societies of 1818 to 1823, and were introduced to the members on October 24, 1831. A committee had gone carefully into the matter and recommended them at a meeting in the Rotunda. John Cleave read the resolutions which were as follows:

To the National Union. We, your Committee, hereby inform you that, in order that this Society may be a real Union, and not a mere chaos, we propose—

1. That you should appoint class leaders for the different districts of the metropolis and its vicinity.

2. That there should be on an average twenty-five members to each class, so that there may be forty class leaders to 1,000 members.

3. That every member should call, or leave his name at the residence of his class leader, once a week, or the class leader on the members, if more convenient.

4. That the list of class leaders be read over in the first general meeting of the Union every month, and, that each class leader be then either continued, or changed, according to the meeting.

5. That each class leader shall keep a list of the names, and residences of the different individuals, who leave their names with him, and that he shall receive their monthly subscription and send it to the secretary.

6. That the services of the class leaders be perfectly gratuitous.

7. That the class leaders constitute a committee, which shall meet once every week at such times and place as shall be deemed most convenient.

8. That all the branches of this Union, who adopt the resolutions submitted to them by this committee, be requested to send class leaders to this meeting, at the rate of one person to twenty-five members, on Friday evening, November 4, at eight o'clock.

Daniel O'Connell who was at the meeting supported the committee and added "the organization recommended, was the same as that which was so successfully followed and pursued by the Wesleyans, and he thought the same sauce that so well answered the goose, might with a certainty be applied to the gander." William Benbow, as chairman, also approved of the resolutions and remarked, "if they wished to judge of the comparative value of any measure by its effects, they had only to refer to the Methodist body as a practical illustration of the Wesleyan rules and regulations." He also expressed the hope "that in a few days London alone would produce from 500 to a thousand such leaders—each at the head of twenty-five men." *"He had no hesitation in saying that if the Union of the Working Classes followed up the plan laid down and established by Wesley—, they would in one short year be able to build themselves a Rotunda to meet at and debate, and enable them to laugh at their enemies, as well as to establish the liberties of their country."* The recommendations of the committee were apparently accepted by the union, for class meetings became a part of the constitution. In the published "Objects and Laws" of the movement it was decided that the general committee should "be empowered to nominate to the Union, for its approval or rejection, a list of such persons as may be recommended to them as fit for class leaders or collectors to the amount of one for every twenty-five members of the Union." Once a fortnight the members of the committee had to "meet the class leaders or collectors" in order "to receive the subscriptions or collections of the members, and see them handed over to the Treasurer." "The class leaders or collectors" were expected to "call upon the members on their list (or the members on them, as may be most convenient) once a week, to receive the contributions; which list they shall make up, and hand over the monies received at their fortnightly meetings to the General Committee." By the month of November, 1831, twenty-four class leaders had been appointed and their names placed on record. At another meeting in the Rotunda, Benbow "recommended them to join classes and propagate the class system. There were 500 and upwards already formed and he believed these would soon be 1,000."

William Lovett, when writing an account of the National Union of Working Classes, asserted that "the most useful of their meetings were the classes. . . . There was a meeting of the class leaders every fortnight attended by the secretary, and to him each class leader paid the two weeks money he had received. The class leader was supplied with authenticated cards of admission; each of these cards authorized the person who took one, on payment of sixpence, to attend the class for three months."

"The class meetings were generally held at the house of some member. The class leader was the chairman and some subject, either for conversation or discussion, was selected. Sometimes selections were made from books. The works of Paine—Godwin—Owen—Ensor—and other Radical writers were preferred. The unstamped periodicals of the day were also subjects of conversation and discussion, and in this manner hundreds of persons were made acquainted with books and principles of which they were previously ignorant. They were made more social, also, and better disposed towards one another. In addition to these useful attainments the conversations and discussions generated and encouraged the talent for public speaking, so useful in a country of corruptions and abuses of all kinds, whence its exercise become a duty."

It is perfectly clear from the evidence available that the class system became an essential part of the organization of the National Union of Working Classes and that it was copied from the Methodists. When the Select Committee met in the early part of 1833 to consider the conduct of Policeman Popay in relation to the private meetings of the National Union of Working Classes, James Brown, a class leader, admitted that their union was divided into classes. The classes were twenty-five in number. They consider as working men that they produce all the wealth of the nation and therefore they ought to be represented in the House of Commons. "This is the nature of our conversation," he frankly declares. "We read newspapers and proceedings in Parliament and comment upon them." "A man may join that class where his friends reside." Any person who desires to join the union "gives his name, his address and his occupation, and he is registered in the class paper . . . then he receives a card, and that always recognizes him as a member." "The person who holds the paper sheet" sees that every man's name and subscription are put down. "He is called the class leader, just in the same way as the Wesleyan Methodists do; that is how the mode originated." "We meet as friends and brothers to lighten each other's minds." . . .

Viewed from the religious standpoint, Methodism in the first half of the nineteenth century can be described as a very popular movement among the working classes of this country. That is one of the conclusions to be derived from a study of the available material. Taking the data of numbers alone the conclusion is inevitable. In spite of conflict and division within, together with opposition from various sources without, the registered members of 1850 were six times greater than in 1800. No other movement at the time showed such a continuous success. While it had practically no effect upon the upper portions of the community, its influence on the lower sections was almost phenomenal.

Another conclusion about which one can be certain is the main cause of its popularity. It captured the affections of the common people because of its religious appeal. Through its agency a panacea for all their troubles was gratuitously offered them, and they accepted it with whole-hearted enthusiasm. Having won so many by its religious appeal, it retained and utilized the majority of them by its collective and democratic customs. By offering opportunities for service it created a sense of individual and communal responsibility. That sense of accountability was never lost while the members had a share in the enterprise. Methodism indeed was much more a layman's movement than a minister's. The Wesleyan preachers might endeavour to appropriate to themselves all the power of legislation and administration, but in the long run they had to yield to the growing demands of the democratic elements within their borders.

Looked at from the sociological standpoint, Methodism presented a clear example of a dualistic tendency. On the one hand it emphasized the importance of the individual, and on the other it illustrated the utility of the collective enterprise. According to John Wesley's teaching, the individual and not society was accountable to the Divine Lord for the way in which personal powers and talents were used. No arbitrary or natural grouping of individuals into a community could obliterate that personal sense of responsibility. In that way Methodism may be described as an individualistic movement. But it was also social. John Wesley stoutly maintained that the religion which he propagated was a social religion. He would have nothing to do with the monastic type of religious exercises. In harmony with this view he organized his followers into groups, and called them classes. He formed the classes into societies, and the societies into circuits, which in turn were made into districts. All the districts were made into one whole and called the "Connexion." Methodism thus became a collective movement. Although John Wesley might be regarded by many as "a benevolent autocrat," his greatest achievement was in the realm of collective activity. He taught his disciples the art of working together. Long before the days of industrial and political collectivity, Methodism developed a highly successful type of religious collectivism. The success becomes all the more astounding when the nature of human material to be utilized is truly visualized. Before the majority of the Methodist recruits could be used in a collective capacity they had to learn discipline, self-control, and even self-sacrifice.

A similar dualism is detected when the movement is regarded from the political standpoint. All the writers of Methodist history readily recognize the autocratic features of John Wesley's system. The Wesleyan Conference was exceedingly authoritative. By its pronouncements on politics it has rightly earned the name of "reactionary" and "conservative." While the extent of its Tory influence may be over-estimated

both by its friends and critics, one ought to remember that it did not always speak for the whole of Methodism. It did not represent the democratic elements inside Wesleyanism. Neither did it represent the democratic sections of the other Methodist sects. These sects could not belie their origin. They were formed on democratic principles, and as their numbers increased a religious democracy developed. Let it be said quite clearly that during our period the democratic elements were always more potent than the autocratic. This factor, associated with the religious appeal, attracted and retained within the Methodist borders large sections of the working-class community. Although Methodism always remained a religious movement, its influence could not be confined to the narrow limits created by its leading preachers. It went beyond the artificial restrictions and filtered to the industrial and political activities of its members. When no other example of collective endeavour presented itself to the working classes, Methodism became a pattern and parent for their democratic exercises and idealism. The Methodist leaders had planned otherwise. But the foolishness of some provideth wisdom for the many.

JUSTIN McCARTHY (1830–1912), journalist, novelist, and historian, was born in Ireland and educated privately because as a Roman Catholic he could not take a university degree in Ireland. His life spanned the period of the great nineteenth-century constitutional reforms, during the latter years of which he was active in politics and several times sat for Parliament from Irish constituencies. In addition to many novels, he wrote several historical works on the politics and political personalities of nineteenth-century Britain. In the last volume of his *History of Our Own Times* (1905) he called Victoria's reign "one of the most important epochs in the whole history of the modern world" which opened an "era in the progress of human life." In this selection written fifty years after passage of the Reform Bill he praises it for settling vital constitutional issues but, like Trevelyan, sees it only as a step in a continuing process of gradual reform.*

Important Constitutional Principles Established

The House of Lords, in yielding without further struggle, settled a principle without which our constitutional system could now hardly continue to work. They settled the principle that the House of Lords were never to carry resistance to any measure coming from the Commons beyond a certain point—beyond the time when it became unmistakably evident that the Commons were in earnest. Since that day no serious attempt has been made by the House of Lords to carry resistance to the popular will any further than just such a period as will allow the House of Commons to reconsider their former decision. When the House of Commons have reconsidered their decision and still adhere to it, it is now almost as clearly settled as any other principle in our constitutional system that the House of Lords are then to give way and withdraw all further opposition. It may be stated in plain words, that were the House of Lords now to depart from this implied arrangement, some modification of our constitutional system, as regards the Upper Chamber, would be inevitable. Another question settled we may hope for ever by the pressure brought

* From Justin McCarthy, *The Epoch of Reform, 1830–1850* (London: Longmans, Green & Co., Ltd., 1882), pp. 74–80.

to bear upon King William, was that which concerns the influence of the Sovereign's own personal will in legislation. The King gave way to the advice of his Ministers on a matter of vital importance to the nation, and on which his opinions were opposed to those of the majority. He yielded, not to mere argument or to mere persuasion, but to actual pressure. It became thereby settled that the personal will of the Sovereign was no longer to be a decisive authority in our scheme of Government. That was, we believe, the last time when the question ever was tested. With the close of the reign of William IV and the accession of Queen Victoria to the throne, ended that chapter of our history in which the personal will of the Sovereign made one of the conditions under which the country is to be governed. It is now satisfactorily, and we trust finally settled, that the Sovereign always yields to the advice of the Ministers. As in the case of the House of Lords so in the case of the Crown, it may be said that any departure from this well-established and well-recognised principle, could we suppose such a thing possible, would now lead beyond doubt to some important modification of our whole constitutional system.

Some alterations . . . were introduced into the reform scheme in the course of its long struggle through both Houses of Parliament. But its main features underwent no material change. To us, looking back on the Reform Bill from this distance of time, it seems that nothing could have been more moderate and even modest in its proposals. Not that the change effected by it was not great. It amounted in truth to something like a parliamentary revolution. But there were certain distinct objects necessary to be accomplished if Parliament was to

remain any longer in harmony with the spirit of the country, and in a condition to deal with its political wants, and it is not easy to see how this change could have been effected in a more cautious and a more gradual way. What the Reform Bill actually did was to pass sentence on the system of close or nomination boroughs, to establish in practical working order the principle that the House of Commons was a representative assembly, bearing due proportion in its numbers and in its arrangement to the numbers and the interests of the constituents, and to extend the suffrage so as to enfranchise the great bulk of the middle and lower middle classes of the community. The Reform Act was indeed very far from bringing representation and constituency into anything like exact proportion, but it made a distinct advance in that way, and it established a principle which it left to be wrought into a more perfect system by future generations. The Bill was only a compromise, but under all the circumstances it could hardly have been anything else. Lord Grey and his colleagues might have brought in a very modest measure of reform, some such scheme as other reformers were frequently bringing forward during the long dull interval when the question was not occupying the attention of any Government. Such a Bill, however, would have been almost as difficult to pass as that which they at last succeeded in carrying into law. On the other hand they might have endeavoured to satisfy the demands of the more Radical members of the House of Commons and of Radicals generally out of doors, and introduced a measure at once bold and comprehensive which would have settled the question for many generations. But we doubt very much whether it would have been possible to carry such a Bill just then. Certainly it would have involved the risk of a most serious struggle, perhaps of something like a warfare of class against class. Lord Grey attempted no uprooting of ancient institutions, and he carried with him what may be called the common sense and common instincts of the great bulk of the English population, in proceeding strictly on what were since his time called the old lines of the constitution. But it is certain that the Bill disappointed a great many not only outside the House of Commons but within it, and we may add not only outside the Government but even in the Cabinet itself. Its one main defect . . . was the manner in which it left the great body of the working classes entirely outside what was called the pale of the constitution. It redeemed the political power of the State from being the monopoly of one great class, and made it the partnership of two great classes. That was an advance in itself, and it established the principle which made further advance possible. But it disappointed those who found themselves not better off but even worse off as regards the franchise than they had been before.

It is clear that the Bill was above all things one which it would have been wise on the part of the Conservatives to accept with as little resistance as possible. It was the most moderate measure of reform which it was possible for any really reforming government to offer, or which would have been accepted by the people at large. It ought, one would think, to have been clear even then to an intelligent Conservative, that the country would never again be content to listen to any smaller project of reform. Yet the Conservatives had not the

slightest idea of accepting any compromise. On the contrary, they had strong hopes that they would be able to resist the whole reform movement and beat it back. There were Tories who not only believed that the Government would never be able to carry any Reform Bill, but were even satisfied that the leaders of the Government did not expect to succeed. Sir James Graham was spoken to by a member in the lobby on the night after the first Reform Bill had been explained. The member who addressed him complimented him and his colleagues on their courage and honesty, but added that he supposed of course they were perfectly prepared to go out of office the next day.

In the course of one of the closing debates on the Reform Bill in the House of Commons, Lord John Russell made use of certain words which were often afterwards cited against him. They were quoted by extreme reformers to his reproach, and they were quoted by extreme opponents of reform as a Ministerial pledge against further change. Lord John Russell said, that in his opinion "so far as Ministers are concerned, this is a final measure. I declared on the second reading of the Reform Bill that if only a part of the measure were carried it would lead to new agitations, but that is now avoided by the state in which the Bill has come from the other House." It was instantly assumed by the extreme advocates of reform that Lord John Russell meant by these words to express his opinion that the era of reform had closed in England, that enough had been done in the way of change for all time, that the political system of this country was then the good made perfect. On the other hand, when many years after Lord John Russell undertook further schemes of reform, the extreme opponents of change accused him of having broken a solemn pledge. The speech was constantly referred to as Lord John Russell's "finality" declaration, and indeed the noble lord himself was irreverently dubbed by certain critics "finality Jack." The meaning, however, of Lord John Russell's statement is perfectly obvious, nor was there anything in it inconsistent with his taking up further schemes of reform at a distant period. What he meant was that as regarded that particular chapter of reform, Lord Grey's government felt that it had closed. They had done enough for the time. They knew very well that in English politics reforms are made in eras or in sections, and that the country will not stand the making of fresh changes year after year. The habit of the English people is to lay in a stock of reform which they believe will last a certain time, and to have no more to do with the question until the time seems to have nearly run out. Any practical politician would have seen that no matter how great might be the class grievances left unremedied by the Reform Bill of 1832, it would be impossible to induce Parliament and the public to set about a new scheme of reform immediately after. Lord John Russell meant, therefore, as indeed he said in plain words, that the government of Lord Grey regarded themselves as having done their part in the settlement of reform, and that having accomplished so much they did not propose to attempt anything further. Lord John Russell, it seems almost needless to say, continued to be as steady an advocate of reform, after the passing of Lord Grey's Bill, as he had been before. He knew well that the Bill was but a beginning and a compromise, and that much more remained to be done even in his own time. He could not be supposed to shut his eyes to the fact that that artisan class, with whom he had always shown much sympathy, were not only still left out of the franchise, but were, indeed, deprived of special franchises and political privileges which they had before the passing of the Bill. No one of Lord John Russell's political sagacity could have failed to see that the enfranchisement of the working class would become "a burning question" before many years should have gone over the heads of statesmen.

The following selection from O. F. CHRISTIE (1867–1953) presents a regretful view of reform, colored by nostalgia for a world beyond recall. Educated at Clifton College, of which he wrote a history, and Trinity College, Oxford, Christie was called to the bar of the Inner Temple in 1892. He combined in later years the professions of barrister, brewer, and writer. With the exception of a pamphlet, *Licensing Practice*, which appeared in 1898, however, his books were published late in his life. Two on nineteenth-century politics, *The Transition from Aristocracy* (1927) and *The Transition to Democracy* (1934), appeared when he was past sixty. Compare his interpretation of the aftereffects of reform with the fears of the Tories in 1832 reported by Marriott.*

▶ The Vices of Democracy Lamented

"But you might have heard a pin drop as Duncannon read the numbers. Then again the shouts broke out, and many of us shed tears. I could scarcely refrain. And the jaw of Peel fell; and the face of Twiss was as the face of a damned soul; and Herries looked like Judas taking his necktie off for the last operation." So wrote Macaulay to Ellis of the division of 22nd March 1831, when the Second Reading of the Reform Bill was carried by a majority of one; but it was not till 7th June of the following year that the Bill, twice altered, became law. The last scene in the House of Lords, when it received the Royal assent, was in utter contrast with that described by Macaulay. In Samuel Reynolds's paint-ing the Government benches are full, the Tory benches are empty; almost alone on the left of the Throne stands the Duke of Sussex, the Whig son of George the Third. One has an impression of the calm and gloom that are appropriate to "The Tapestry." Between these two dates the hopes and fears of the Bill's champions and opposers had risen and fallen. In the country there had been terrible riots, in London incessant intrigue; but the Zenobias of Mayfair had exerted themselves in vain. The King had wavered; Earl Grey had resigned; the Duke had been obliged to advise his recall. During eleven fateful days of May 1832 England had been on the brink of revolution.

* From O. F. Christie, *The Transition from Aristocracy, 1832–1867* (New York: G. Putnam's Sons, 1928), pp. 35–36, 42–45, 57–62. Reprinted by permission of Seeley Service & Co., Ltd., London.

Macaulay, in likening one Tory to a devil and another to Judas, gives proof—if proof were needed—of the violent political passions of the day and of how ardently he himself entertained them. Party feeling poisoned even his kindly temperament, and (what was less excusable) his literary criticism. Not content with hating Croker as a political opponent, he virulently attacked him as a man of letters. It was in September 1831, in the very height of the Reform struggle, that his criticism of Croker's Boswell appeared in *The Edinburgh Review*: "A dog of the House of Montague moves me. . . . I will take the wall of any man or maid of Montague's." But Macaulay did not exaggerate the consternation in the Tory ranks. And yet, perhaps, it is necessary for us to call to mind what the Tories stood to lose, in order fully to understand, and indeed to sympathize, with their apprehensions. . . .

The Tories fought against Reform, firstly for selfish and personal reasons, because it affected their fortunes and careers; and yet this latter fear—the fear of the loss of an honourable career—was by no means an ignoble motive. But there was another thing they feared, which no man may blame them for fearing, and that was Revolution,

"The dark, unbottom'd, infinite abyss"

which they believed to be yawning in front of them. It was the unknown future that they apprehended, of an England with a new kind of government that would represent forces incalculable and immeasurable. They feared, in fact, the destruction of Monarchy, House of Lords, and Church, and all the ancient preservative institutions of the country.

These fears of some terrible cataclysm had been felt long before Reform had come within the range of practical politics. In 1809 (we read in Creevey) "Charles Warren the lawyer predicts the present reign will end quietly from the popularity of the King, but that when it ends, the profligacy and unpopularity of the Princes with the situation of the country as to financial difficulties, and the rapidly and widely extended growth of Methodism, will produce a storm." In 1812 Creevey himself writes: "The more one sees of the conduct of this most singular man (the Prince Regent), the more one becomes convinced he is doomed, from his personal character, to shake his throne." Greville . . . was moved by the condition of the poor in Sunderland and Rotherhithe, and by revelations made at an Old Bailey trial, to the gloomiest prognostications. And we may take it as certain that since the French Revolution, which (according to Burke) had affected one-fifth of the population with subversive ideas, vague apprehensions had been endemic. These fears now centred round the Reform agitation. Some were alarmed at the prospect, if the Bill should pass; some, if it should be rejected. Macaulay claimed "that the question, whether the change in itself be good or bad, has become a question of secondary importance; that, good or bad, the thing must be done; that a law as strong as the laws of attraction and motion has decreed it" (House of Commons, 10th November 1831). Whether the Bill were passed or rejected, it seemed as if terrible results were to be expected.

In the great towns the "Mob"—the unknown or little-known *residuum* of the population—had always been a formidable monster. In London it had shown its power in the Sacheverell riots and the Wilkes riots; at the Gordon Riots it had

72796

poured out of its fastnesses—the Minories, the Dials, the Mint, and the purlieus of the Fleet—and for a time held the City at its mercy. But these riots had been urban, and had been occasioned by political and religious rather than by social grievances; there had been no real *jacquerie* in England since the Peasants' Revolt of 1377. In the winter of 1830–1831 many counties in England did experience something very like a *jacquerie*. "This part of the country," wrote Mrs. Edward Bulwer (on 5th December 1830), from Heydon in Norfolk, "like every other, has been in a terrible state of disturbance. Meetings of five or six hundred desperadoes in every village. About ten days ago there was a meeting of this sort at a place called Reepham, which all the noblemen and gentlemen in the county went to try and put down, by telling the people that their wrongs should be redressed, their wages raised, and employment given to them. Upon which the mob shouted: "It is very well to try and talk us over, but we will have blood for our suppers!" They then began pelting the magistrates and gentlemen with large stones. . . . The burnings are dreadful, but every house in this part of the world is in a state of defence, and all the farmers, shopkeepers, servants, etc., etc., sworn in special constables." By the middle of December incendiary fires were burning in thirteen counties, and the Government appointed a special Commission to try the incendiaries. Of the Rotundanists, so called from their place of weekly assembly in Blackfriars Bridge Road, Place himself said: "Among these men were some who were perfectly atrocious, whose purpose was riot, as providing an opportunity for plundering." At Bristol the Bishop's Palace, public buildings **and** many private

houses were burnt to the ground. At Nottingham the Castle and several factories were burnt. In Darlington a lady driving beside Lord Tankerville was nearly killed by a paving stone that was hurled at her. The house of Mrs. Musters in Nottinghamshire was burnt; she had to pass the night out of doors in the damp and died of exposure. There was said to exist a scheme to seize the families of certain peers and hold them for hostages. . . .

Thanks to Reform the danger of civil war was averted. And yet, although this prime object was attained, and although everywhere there was great public rejoicing, it is easy to understand the apprehensions with which the great event of 1832 was regarded by all who had a "stake" in the country. In 1688 Divine Right was discredited, and the King who claimed it was driven into exile. "What we did at the Revolution," said Johnson in his old age, "was necessary, but it broke our Constitution." Burke maintained, on the contrary, that it cured a "peccant" part of our Constitution which was thereby brought to a state of perfection; and the Tories of 1832, whatever they still thought of 1688, had become Burkeites in this sense—that they believed that any change at all would now be for the worse. "If I had imposed on me the duty of framing a legislature for any country," said the Duke of Wellington in the House of Lords (2nd November 1830), "I do not mean to assert that I could form such a legislature as you possess now, for the nature of man is incapable of recasting such excellence at once, but my great endeavour would be to form some description of legislature which would produce the same results." So of 1832 the Duke and his high Tory followers would have said what Johnson said of 1688—that what was done then was necessary, but that it "broke our Constitution." The nation was moving from the known to the unknown. A venerable lady who died quite recently, and yet could remember those days, has written: "The floodgates were opened in 1832, and never since has the current stopped." This was the favourite metaphor of Sir Leicester Dedlock, whom Dickens presented as the type of the stupid reactionary Tory; but can anyone now say whither the current is carrying us? It is true that the fears which Macaulay had ridiculed were duly falsified. No Marats, no Santerres appeared in the House of Commons; it has been reserved for our own day to see therein members who openly advocate a violent revolution. By 1835 even the high Tory Gladstone could take a sanguine view of the situation: "To think that notwithstanding the Ten-Pound Clause a moderate Parliament may be returned; in fine, to believe that we have now *some* prospect of surviving the *Reform* Bill without a bloody revolution, is to me as surprising as delightful; it seems to me the greatest and most providential mercy with which a nation was ever visited." Nevertheless, since 1832, wise and thoughtful Englishmen have been continually obessed by forebodings as to the stability of our social order. If France has never had a stable Government since 1789, England has never been free from political uneasiness since 1832. In 1842 armed mobs destroyed factories; Stockport was plundered and part of Manchester destroyed; Peel requisitioned arms to protect his country house. In 1846 Croker (writing to Brougham) prophesies that, after a period of anarchy, "we shall have a federal republic after the American fashion." It was Gladstone's opinion that

there would have been a revolution if the Corn Laws had not been repealed. In 1848 Matthew Arnold writes from London: "It will be *rioting* here, only; still, the hour of the hereditary peerage and eldest sonship and immense properties has, I am convinced, as Lamartine would say, struck. . . . Carlyle gives our institutions, as they are called, aristocracy, Church, etc., five years, I heard last night." In this year houses in the West End of London were put in a state of fortification. In 1850 Stanley writes to Croker, with reference to the next General Election: "If this or any Free Trade Government *then* acquire a majority, the game is up; and I firmly believe we shall be in a rapid progress towards a republic in name as well as reality. . . . We are falling into the fatal sleep which precedes mortification and death." Henry Drummond to Croker (1853): "I say that Bright is right, and we are on the eve of becoming a Republic." Carlyle (*Journal*, 1866): "Sometimes I think the tug of revolution struggle may be even *near* for poor England, much nearer than I once judged—very questionable to me whether England won't go quite to *smash* under it." Shaftesbury to Granville (1868): "Be assured, my dear friend, that no merely human skill will save the British Empire from utter shipwreck." I will conclude with a wail from Beaconsfield, who so rarely desponded, in a letter written to Lord John Manners in December 1880: "And yet I see no prospect of salvation, and really believe that you, at least, will live long enough to see the crown fall from our gracious Sovereign's head."

I could quote, if it were necessary, sad vaticinations to which many other personages have given utterance since 1832, men so diverse as Harrowby, Hobhouse, Wellington, Greville, Salisbury, Dr. Arnold, Bagehot, Lowe and Peel. The fear common to all of them arises from a deep-seated conviction that government can only be properly carried on by the few and not by the many. But this is a doctrine which, since Reform, could not be preached from a platform by any politician who valued his career. It has been more and more necessary for anyone who aspires to political success to pay compliments to democracy, and no doubt many of these compliments have been sincere. Yet the most sincere believers have become disillusioned. Lord Morley, towards the close of his long life, asked: "As for progress, what signs of it are there now? And all the Victorians believed in it from the Utilitarians onwards."

At least we may say that the fears of a cataclysm have not yet been fulfilled. Our social order still stands unbroken, and we have much that may hearten us to look the doubtful future in the face. In writing of a period of transition one may also remark that the men whose gloomy prophecies I have quoted, and who were not fools, were nearly all survivors from the previous age—an age which was so far from taking the virtues of representatives government for granted that it regarded "democracy" as almost certainly connoting revolution. Democracy was associated with the excesses of the French Revolution, and that revolution was almost as near to the men of 1830–1832 as Queen Victoria's first Jubilee is to ourselves. "A perfect democracy," wrote Burke, "is the most shameless thing in the world"—because it is absolute and unrestrained. Croker continued of the same opinion in 1845: "The *facilis descensus Averni*—that is Democracy." To the progressive Whig or

Liberal, it is true, Croker stood for reaction and blind pessimism. But Macaulay himself, who detested Croker, said of purely democratic institutions that "they must sooner or later destroy liberty or civilization or both." We have lately heard a cant phrase about "making the world safe *for* Democracy." Our great-grandfathers were preoccupied in making the world safe *from* Democracy. As late as 1865 Disraeli was hoping that the House of Commons would "sanction no step that has a tendency to democracy." Now the Reform Bill was inspired by the same democratic ideal as had inspired the French Revolution. The vote was a Right, one of the Rights of Man, a Right that should be claimed by all, and not (as Disraeli used to argue) a privilege that should be granted only to those who proved they deserved it. Though the Bill enfranchised only 220,000 voters, it recognized the democratic principle of an individual's right to a vote, and that Parliament should be in this sense "representative." But this theory of representation, also, was clean contrary to the doctrine of Burke. "When," he asked, "did you hear in Great Britain of any province suffering from the inequality of its representation; what district from having no representation at all? Not only our monarchy and our peerage secure the equality on which our unity depends, but it is the spirit of the House of Commons itself. . . Cornwall elects as many members as all Scotland, but is Cornwall better taken care of than Scotland? Few trouble their heads about any of your bases, out of some giddy clubs." In 1794 the Attorney-General, prosecuting Thomas Hardy for high treason, described representative government as "The direct contrary of the government which is established here. There was a Tory view held in that day that men should first decide what sort of persons would be their best representatives and then, second, what sort of persons would be most likely to elect them. There may be something to be said for this old-fashioned notion; but it is only necessary here to bear in mind how it contrasts with the later doctrine—that the more numerous the electors the wiser will be the representative.

The Reform Movement in England, says Mr. G. M. Trevelyan, began with the Yorkshire freeholders, afterwards received support from the philosophic Dissenters, and still later from the working classes. Was it also in the end inspired by ideas even more subversive than those of Paine and Hardy?

E. P. THOMPSON (1924–   ) is a member of the new generation of English historians of the working class. Following military service in World War II, he studied at Cambridge and subsequently worked in adult education. He is presently at the University of Warwick. Besides the book from which this selection is drawn, his writing includes a study of William Morris and a volume of political essays. He helped found the magazine *The New Reasoner* and has been chairman of the editorial board of *The New Left Review*. Here he traces the emergence of a working class self-consciousness, the culmination of which he believes came with the exclusion of the workers from political participation in 1832.*

Class Consciousness of the Working People Achieved

"A Sort of Machine"

"The present mischief these two men [Owen and Hodgskin] have in some respects done is incalculable," noted Francis Place. The "mischief" is written across the years 1831–5. And at this point the limits of this study have been reached; for there is a sense in which the working class is no longer in the making, but has been made. To step over the threshold, from 1832 to 1833, is to step into a world in which the working-class presence can be felt in every county in England, and in most fields of life.

The new class consciousness of working people may be viewed from two aspects. On the one hand, there was a consciousness of the identity of interests between working men of the most diverse occupations and levels of attainment, which was embodied in many institutional forms, and which was expressed on an unprecedented scale in the general unionism of 1830–4. This consciousness and these institutions were only to be found in fragmentary form in the England of 1780.

On the other hand, there was a consciousness of the identity of the interests of the working class, or "productive classes," *as against* those of other classes; and within this there was ma-

* From *The Making of the English Working Class*, by E. P. Thompson, pp. 807–812, 826–828, 830–832. © Copyright 1963 by E. P. Thompson. Reprinted by permission of Victord Gollancz, Ltd., and Pantheon Books, a Division of Random House, Inc., New York. Footnotes omitted.

turing the claim for an alternative *system*. But the final definition of this class consciousness was, in large part, the consequence of the response to working-class strength of the middle class. The line was drawn, with extreme care, in the franchise qualifications of 1832. It had been the peculiar feature of English development that, where we would expect to find a growing middle-class reform movement, with a working-class tail, only later succeeded by an independent agitation of the working class, in fact this process was reversed. The example of the French Revolution had initiated three simultaneous processes: a panic-struck counter-revolutionary response on the part of the landed and commercial aristocracy; a withdrawal on the part of the industrial bourgeoisie and an accommodation (on favourable terms) with the *status quo*; and a rapid radicalisation of the popular reform movement until the Jacobin cadres who were tough enough to survive through the Wars were in the main little masters, artisans, stockingers and croppers, and other working men. The twenty-five years after 1795 may be seen as the years of the "long counter-revolution"; and in consequence the Radical movement remained largely working-class in character, with an advanced democratic "populism" as its theory. But the triumph of such a movement was scarcely to be welcomed by the mill-owners, iron-masters, and manufacturers. Hence the peculiarly repressive and anti-egalitarian ideology of the English middle classes (Godwin giving way to Bentham, Bentham giving way to Malthus, M'Culloch, and Dr. Ure, and these giving rise to Baines, Macaulay and Edwin Chadwick) Hence also the fact that the mildest measure of reform, to meet the evident irrationalities of Old Corruption, was actually *delayed*, by the resistance of the old order on the one hand, and the timidity of the manufacturers on the other.

The Reform Bill crisis of 1832—or, to be more accurate, the successive crises from early in 1831 until the "days of May" in 1832—illustrates these theses at almost every point. The agitation arose from "the people" and rapidly displayed the most astonishing consensus of opinion as to the imperative necessity for "reform." Viewed from one aspect, England was without any doubt passing through a crisis in these twelve months in which revolution was possible. The rapidity with which the agitation extended indicates the degree to which experience in every type of constitutional and quasi-legal agitation was present among the people:

The systematic way in which the people proceeded, their steady perseverance, their activity and skill astounded the enemies of reform. Meetings of almost every description of persons were held in cities, towns, and parishes; by journeymen tradesmen in their clubs, and by common workmen who had no trade clubs or associations of any kind. . . .

So Place wrote of the autumn of 1830, adding (of February 1831):

. . . yet there was not even the smallest communication between places in the same neighbourhood; each portion of the people appeared to understand what ought to be done. . . .

"The great majority" of those who attended the swelling demonstrations, the King's private Secretary complained in March 1831 to Grey, "are of the very lowest class." The enormous demonstrations, rising to above 100,000 in Birmingham and London in the autumn of 1831 and May 1832, were overwhelmingly composed of artisans and working men.

"We did not cause the excitement about reform," Grey wrote a little pee-vishly to the King, in March 1831: "We found it in full vigour when we came into office." And, viewed from another aspect, we can see why throughout these crisis months a revolution was in fact improbable. The reason is to be found in the very strength of the work-ing-class Radical movement; the skill with which the middle-class leaders, Brougham, *The Times*, the *Leeds Mer-cury* both used this threat of working-class force, and negotiated a line of re-treat acceptable to all but the most die-hard defenders of the *ancien régime*; and the awareness on the part of the Whigs and the least intransigent Tories that, while Brougham and Baines were only blackmailing them, nevertheless if a compromise was not come to, the mid-dle-class reformers might no longer be able to hold in check the agitation at their backs.

The industrial bourgeoisie desired, with heart and soul, that a revolution should not take place, since they knew that on the very day of its commence-men there would be a dramatic process of radicalisation, in which Huntite, trade unionist, and Owenite leaders would command growing support in nearly all the manufacturing centres. "Threats of a 'revolution' are employed by the middle classes and petty mas-ters," wrote the *Poor Man's Guardian*. But—

a violent revolution is not only beyond the means of those who threaten it, but is to them their greatest object of alarm; for they know that such a revolution can only be effected by the poor and despised millions, who, if excited to the step, might use it for their own advantage, as well as for that of

themselves, who would thus . . . have their dear rights of property endangered: be assured that a violent revolution is their greatest dread. . . .

The middle-class reformers fought skill-fully on both fronts. On the one hand *The Times* came forward as the actual organiser of mass agitation: "We trust there is not a county, town, or village in the United Kingdom which will not meet and petition for a reform. . . ." It even urged upon the people "the solemn duty of forming themselves into po-litical societies throughout the whole realm." It supported—as did Edward Baines, before cheering throngs, at Leeds—measures of enforcement which led directly on towards revolution: the run on the Banks, refusal to pay taxes, and the arming of members of Political Unions. On the other hand, the riots at Nottingham, Derby and Bristol in Oc-tober 1831 underlined the dual function of the Political Unions on the Birming-ham model:

These Unions were to be for the promotion of the cause of reform, for the protection of life and property against the detailed but irregular outrages of the mob, as well as for the maintenance of *other* great interests against the systematic violences of an oligarchy. . . .

These middle-class incendiaries car-ried in their knapsacks a special con-stable's baton. There were occasions when the Tories themselves hoped to outwit them, by encouraging the inde-pendent working-class reform move-ment to display itself in a form so alarm-ing that Brougham and Baines would run to Old Corruption for protection. When the National Union of the Work-ing Classes proposed to call a demon-stration in London for manhood suf-frage, and in resistance to the Whig Reform Bill, the King himself wrote (4 November 1831):

His Majesty is by no means displeased that the measures contemplated by the meeting in question are so violent, and . . . objectionable, as he trusts that the manifestation of such intentions and such purposes may afford the opportunity . . . of checking the progress of the Political Unions. . . .

Throughout the country middle-class and working class reformers manoeuvred for control of the movement. In the earliest stages, until the summer of 1831, the middle-class Radicals held the advantage. Seven years before Wooler had closed the *Black Dwarf* with a sadly disillusioned final Address. There was (in 1824) no "public devotedly attached to the cause of parliamentary reform." Where hundreds and thousands had once clamoured for reform, it now seemed to him that they had only "clamoured for bread"; the orators and journalists of 1816–20 had only been "bubbles thrown up in the fermentation of society." Many of the working-class leaders of the late 1820s shared his disillusion, and accepted the anti-political stance of their master, Owen. It was not until the summer of 1830, with the rural labourers' "revolt" and the July Revolution in France, that the tide of popular interest began to turn back to political agitation. And thenceforward the insanely stubborn last-ditch resistance of the die-hards (the Duke of Wellington, the Lords, the Bishops) to *any* measure of reform dictated a strategy (which was exploited to the full by the middle-class Radicals) by which popular agitation was brought to bear behind Grey and Russell, and in support of a Bill from which the majority had nothing to gain.

Thus the configuration of forces of 1816–20 (and, indeed, of 1791–4), in which the popular demand for Reform was identified with Major Cartwright's platform of manhood suffrage, was broken up. "If any persons suppose that this Reform will lead to ulterior measures," Grey declared in the House in November 1831:

they are mistaken; for there is no one more decided against annual parliaments, universal suffrage, and the ballot, than I am. My object is not to favour, but to put an end to such hopes and projects.

This was clearly enough seen by the older Radicals, the majority of whose articulate spokesmen poured scorn on the Whig Bill until the final "days of May." "It mattered not to him," declared a Macclesfield Radical, "whether he was governed by a boroughmonger, or a whoremonger, or a cheesemonger, if the system of monopoly and corruption was still to be upheld." Hunt, from his place as Member for Preston (1830–2), maintained the same propositions, in only slightly more decorous language. George Edmonds, the witty and courageous Radical schoolmaster, who had chaired Birmingham's first great post-war demonstration on Newhall Hill (January 1817), declared:

I am not a house-holder—I can, on a push, be a musket-holder. The nothing-but-the-Bill does not recognise George Edmonds as a citizen—George Edmonds scorns the nothing-but-the-Bill, except as cut the first at the national robber.

This was the position also of the élite of London's Radical artisans, enrolled in the National Union of Working Classes and Others, whose weekly debates in the Rotunda in 1831 and 1832 were reported in Hetherington's *Poor Man's Guardian*—undoubtedly the finest working-class weekly which had (until that time) been published in Britain. The debates were attended by Hetherington himself (when not in prison), William Lovett, James Watson, John Gast, the brilliant and ill-fated Julian Hibbert, and old William Benbow (the former colleague of Bamford and of Mitchell), now pressing his proposal for a "Grand National Holiday," or month's general strike, in the course of which the productive classes would assume control of the nation's government and resources. The debates increasingly turned upon the definition of class. William Carpenter, who shared with Hetherington the honour of initiating the strugle for the "unstamped" press, offered a dissentient opinion. The Whig Bill ought to be supported, as a "wedge." He complained that the *Poor Man's Guardian* used the words "middle men" and "middle class" as "convertible terms," whereas the middle classes "are not only *not* a class of persons having interests different from your own. They are the *same* class; they are, generally speaking, *working* or *labouring* men." Throughout the entire crisis the controversy continued. After the Bill had passed, the *Poor Man's Guardian* recorded its conclusion:

The promoters of the Reform Bill projected it, not with a view to subvert, or even remodel our aristocratic institutions, but to consolidate them by a reinforcement of sub-aristocracy from the middle-classes. . . . The only difference between the Whigs and the Tories is this—the Whigs would give the shadow to preserve the substance; the Tories would not give the shadow, because stupid as they are, the millions will not stop at shadows but proceed onwards to realities. . . .

The line from 1832 to Chartism is not a haphazard pendulum alternation of "political" and "economic" agitations but a direct progression, in which simul-taneous and related movements converge towards a single point. This point was the vote. There is a sense in which the Chartist movement commenced, not in 1836 with the promulgation of the "Six Points," but at the moment when the Reform Bill received Royal Assent. Many of the provincial Political Unions never disbanded, but commenced at once to agitate against the "shopocrat" franchise. In January 1833 the *Working Man's Friend* was able to announce that the fortress of middle-class Radicalism had been stormed: ". . . in spite of all the opposition and chicanery of a RAG MERCHANT MONARCHY, the Midland Union of the Working Classes was formed by the brave, but, till then, misled people of that country." The characteristic ideology of Birmingham Radicalism, which united employers and journeymen in opposition to the aristocracy, the Banks, the National Debt, and the "paper-money system," was beginning to fall apart. For a time Attwood himself was carried with the new current, partly through loyalty to the regiments to which he had made large promises before. Once again, a monster demonstration gathered on Newhall Hill (May 1833), at which an attendance of 180,000 was claimed, and at which there was expressed—

. . . a sentiment of common hatred to the parties whom, having been mainly instrumental in forcing into power, they now assembled to express their disgust of the . . . treachery which they had manifested.

The attendance was swelled by colliers from Walsall, iron-workers from Wolverhampton, outworkers from Dudley. The process of radicalisation which was to make Birmingham a Chartist metropolis had begun.

But the content of this renewed agitation was such that the vote itself implied "much more," and that is why it had to be denied. (The Birmingham of 1833 was not the Birmingham of 1831: it was now the home of an Equitable Labour Exchange, it was the headquarters of the socialist Builders' Union, it housed the editorial office of the *Pioneer*.) The vote, for the workers of this and the next decade, was a symbol whose importance it is difficult for us to appreciate, our eyes dimmed by more than a century of the smog of "two-party parliamentary politics." It implied, first, *égalité*: equality of citizenship, personal dignity, worth. "Instead of bricks, mortar, and dirt, MAN ought to be represented," wrote one pamphleteer, lamenting the lot of "the miserable, so-called 'free-born' Englishman, excluded from the most valuable right that man can enjoy in political society." "Be we, of the working millions," wrote George Edmonds—

never more seen at baby-shows, Lord Mayor penny-peeps, and gingerbread Coronations— be not present as accomplices in such national fooleries. Let the tawdy actors have all the fun to themselves.

"Like the wild Irish of old, the British millions have been too long insolently placed without the pale of social governments":

I now speak the thoughts of my unrepresented fellow millions, the Wild English, the freeborn slaves of the nineteenth century.

But in the context of the Owenite and Chartist years, the claim for the vote implied also further claims: a new way of reaching out by the working people for *social control* over their conditions of life and labour. At first, and inevitably, the exclusion of the working class provoked a contrary rejection, by the working class, of all forms of political action. Owen had long prepared the ground for this, with his indifference to political Radicalism. But in the post-1832 swing to general unionism, this anti-political bias was not quietist but embattled, militant, and even revolutionary. To examine the richness of the political thought of these years would take us further into the history of general unionism—and, indeed, into the early years of Chartism—than we intend to go. They are years in which Benbow canvassed his notion of the "Grand National Holiday" in the industrial districts; in which the printing-worker, John Francis Bray, carried forward Hodgskin's ideas, in lectures to Leeds artisans, later published as *Labour's Wrongs and Labour's Remedies;* in which the Builders' Union and the Grand National Consolidated Trades Union rose and fell; and in which Doherty and Fielden founded the "Society for National Regeneration" with its remedy of the General Strike for the Eight-Hour Day. The Owenite communitarians were fertile with notions and experiments prefiguring advances in the care of children, the relations between the sexes, education, housing, and social policy. Nor were these ideas canvassed among a limited intelligentsia only; building workers, potters, weavers, and artisans were willing, for a while, to risk their livelihood to put experiments to the test. The swarming variety of journals, many of which made exacting demands upon the readers, were addressed to an authentic working-class audience. In the silk mills of the Colden Valley, isolated on the Pennines between Yorkshire and Lancashire, the Owenite journals were read. . . .

This collective self-consciousness was indeed the great spiritual gain of the Industrial Revolution, against which the disruption of an older and in many ways more humanly-comprehensible way of life must be set. It was perhaps a unique formation, this British working class of 1832. The slow, piecemeal accretions of capital accumulation had meant that the preliminaries to the Industrial Revolution stretched backwards for hundreds of years. From Tudor times onwards this artisan culture had grown more complex with each phase of technical and social change. Delaney, Dekker and Nashe: Winstanley and Lilburne: Bunyan and Defoe—all had at times addressed themselves to it. Enriched by the experiences of the 17th century, carrying through the 18th century the intellectual and libertarian traditions which we have described, forming their own traditions of mutuality in the friendly society and trades club, these men did not pass, in one generation, from the peasantry to the new industrial town. They suffered the experience of the Industrial Revolution as articulate, free-born Englishmen. Those who were sent to gaol might know the Bible better than those on the Bench, and those who were transported to Van Diemen's Land might ask their relatives to send Cobbett's *Register* after them.

This was, perhaps, the most distinguished popular culture England has known. It contained the massive diversity of skills, of the workers in metal, wood, textiles and ceramics, without whose inherited "mysteries" and superb ingenuity with primitive tools the inventions of the Industrial Revolution could scarcely have got further than the drawing-board. From this culture of the craftsman and the self-taught there came scores of inventers, organisers, journalists and political theorists of impressive quality. It is easy enough to say that this culture was backward-looking or conservative. True enough, one direction of the great agitations of the artisans and outworkers, continued over fifty years, was to *resist* being turned into a proletariat. When they knew that this cause was lost, yet they reached out again, in the Thirties and Forties, and sought to achieve new and only imagined forms of social control. During all this time they were, as a class, repressed and segregated in their own communities. But what the counter-revolution sought to repress grew only more determined in the quasi-legal institutions of the underground. Whenever the pressure of the rulers relaxed, men came from the petty workshops or the weavers' hamlets and asserted new claims. They were told that they had no rights, but they knew that they were born free. The Yeomanry rode down their meeting, and the right of public meeting was gained. The pamphleteers were gaoled, and from the gaols they edited pamphlets. The trade unionists were imprisoned, and they were attended to prison by processions with bands and union banners.

Segregated in this way, their institutions acquired a peculiar toughness and resilience. Class also acquired a peculiar resonance in English life: everything, from their schools to their shops, their chapels to their amusements, was turned into a battle-ground of class. The marks of this remain, but by the outsider they are not always understood. If we have in our social life little of the tradition of *égalité,* yet the class-consciousness of the working man has little in it of deference. "Orphans we are, and bastards of society," wrote James Morrison in 1834. The tone is not one of resignation but of pride.

Again and again in these years working men expressed it thus: "they wish to make us tools," or "implements," or "machines." A witness before the parliamentary committee enquiring into the hand-loom weavers (1835) was asked to state the view of his fellows on the Reform Bill:

Q. Are the working classes better satisfied with the institutions of the country since the change has taken place?

A. I do not think they are. They viewed the Reform Bill as a measure calculated to join the middle and upper classes to Government, and leave them in the hands of Government as a sort of machine to work according to the pleasure of Government.

Such men met Utilitarianism in their daily lives, and they sought to throw it back, not blindly, but with intelligence and moral passion. They fought, not the machine, but the exploitive and oppressive relationships intrinsic to industrial capitalism. In these same years, the great Romantic criticism of Utilitarianism was running its parallel but altogether separate course. After William Blake, no mind was at home in both cultures, nor had the genius to interpret the two traditions to each other. It was a muddled Mr. Owen who offered to disclose the "new moral world," while Wordsworth and Coleridge had withdrawn behind their own ramparts of disenchantment. Hence these years appear at times to display, not a revolutionary challenge, but a resistance movement, in which both the Romantics and the Radical craftsmen opposed the annunciation of Acquisitive Man. In the failure of the two traditions to come to a point of junction, something was lost. How much we cannot be sure, for we are among the losers.

Yet the working people should not be seen only as the lost myriads of eternity. They had also nourished, for fifty years, and with incomparable fortitude, the Liberty Tree. We may thank them for these years of heroic culture.

This selection is a review of Norman Gash's *Politics in the Age of Peel* and reveals much of the operation of practical politics after 1832. In doing so, it raises some questions about facile generalizations concerning the shift in the center of political gravity after 1832 and the fate of corrupt electoral practices. The review is by W. L. BURN (1904–1966), who was professor of modern history at the University of Newcastle upon Tyne. Also a barrister, he contributed to historical and legal reviews and wrote two books on the British West Indies. His latest work was a study of mid-Victorian society entitled *The Age of Equipoise*. In telling us of Gash's research in this review, he reveals a moderate Tory skepticism about suffrage reform and electoral honesty.*

Politics Under Reform

The political convulsions which shook England between 1830 and 1848 were the symptoms of a confusion which went far deeper. It was as though one generation was being presented at once with every idea, had suddenly become sensitive to every wrong, was feverishly searching for every remedy. It was an age of declamation and denunciation, of febrile enthusiasm and passionate over-statement. Dozens of men and not a few women—Carlyle, Oastler, Newman, Chadwick, Thomas Arnold, J. S. Mill, Harriet Martineau—were ready to demonstrate where the faults lay and how they should be set right. Dogmas were flung between rival groups of contestants like stones in a brawl. Utilitarians, Evangelicals, Tractarians, Chartists, Young Englanders prided themselves on the possession of the single, the supreme solution. It was an age of desperate remedies and grandiose projects, from the People's Charter to the Eglinton Tournament. The possibility of armed violence, of revolution was never very far away. . . . It seemed more than once that society might burst asunder, not so much through its faults and miseries as through its energy and passion and hope.

It did not; and men who had contemplated taking up arms in 1831 turned to making comfortable livings and reading Trollope and the *Saturday Review,* and writing sensible pamphlets

---

* From W. L. Burn, "Political Realism," *Twentieth Century,* vol. CLIV (1953), pp. 127–34. Reprinted by permission of the author and *Twentieth Century.*

on transportation and penal reform. How the wild hopes and the bitterness and the despair of the 'thirties and early 'forties passed into the complacency of the 'fifties would take a long time to explain, if it could be explained at all. One obvious point is that not everyone was light-headed with hope or embittered by despair in the 'thirties; any more than everyone was complacent in the 'fifties. There were always plenty, perhaps a majority, of competent, business-like, not too sensitive or too scrupulous persons, who took the world as they found it and set themselves to squeeze money or power or position out of it. They were not, perhaps, the most admirable of mankind but they conducted into safer channels feelings which, if left to themselves, might have disrupted society. It may be a matter of personal opinion whether it is better to kill and die at a barricade for some incoherent vision of freedom or to take five pounds at the back-door of a beer-house for a vote, but it was as well for the sake of the country that the prevailing belief was in favour of the second of these alternatives.

A book of quite remarkable interest by Mr. Norman Gash[1] seeks

to reconstruct the ordinary working world of the politician . . . to learn what were the political practices as opposed to the constitutional theories or legal machinery of the times; the restraints imposed by supporters as well as by opponents; the peculiar demands of indispensable political techniques; the unceasing conflict between ideal ends and imperfect means; and, most important of all, perhaps, the implicit fundamental attitudes which condition everything but are often unconscious, or are taken for

[1] *Politics in the Age of Peel: a Study in the Technique of Political Representation, 1830–1850.* (London: Longmans, Green & Co., Ltd., 1953).

granted, and are therefore rarely discussed or recorded.

Such enquiries reveal much but they rarely discover heroes. To none of the three men who are among Mr Gash's principal characters could one apply the adjective heroic, but even here one can trace, for good or ill, a certain line of development. Bonham, Peel's party manager, was a gentleman by birth; he had been at Oxford and had been called to the Bar; he held minor office and was liked, as well as used, by some of the most notable men of the day. Joseph Parkes, a Warwickshire man, had been educated at the University of Glasgow and had practised as a solicitor in Birmingham where, in the crisis of the Reform Bill struggle, he had acted as the chief link between the Government and the Political Union. For a moment, when it seemed likely that Wellington would come into office, Parkes was ready to fight—"I and two friends should have made the revolution, whatever the cost"—but he found his proper place as the chief party manager in the Liberal interest, from 1833 to 1847. He was a convinced Radical, the correspondent of Bentham, Place and Grote; but Althorp regarded him as a man to be trusted and even Grey swore that he *would* know him; provoking from his wife the hope that there was no Mrs Parkes.

With all their limitations Bonham and Parkes existed in their own right. They had had some formal education; they had convictions; they came to live in and for politics but they could have lived, not negligibly, outside them. A further turn of the political machine produced James Coppock who had been a haberdasher's clerk and an unsuccessful silk merchant before he became articled to a solicitor and showed his aptitude for electoral organization in 1832. Parkes installed him in 1835 as secretary of the Reform Association and for the next twenty-two years, first in that capacity and later as a parliamentary agent, he built up a reputation which, if it was not altogether enviable, was unique. He travelled far more extensively than Bonham or Parkes; he dipped his hand far more deeply into the cess-pit of "practical politics." He was not the man to leave autobiographical notes—in these days he would have conducted his business by telephone—but we catch glimpses of him here and there: as the defendant to an action for a penalty arising out of bribery in the Ludlow by-election of 1839; taking statements from voters who were prepared, after they had had a talk with him, to swear that they had been bribed by the Conservatives; running for his life (as he alleged) across Parker's Piece, pursued by a Cambridge mob; facing parliamentary committees with a calculated impertinence; fighting election petitions and arranging the necessary compromises behind the scenes. He had his standards: he would deceive a parliamentary committee, but his professional opponents could make a bargain with him and know that it would be kept. After Bonham and Parkes retired, and probably before, he was at the top of his own line of business. The inquiry in 1853 into the Durham City election produced some revealing questions and answers:

Q. "From your experience, I suppose you do not often ask for suggestions?"
A. "I do not, in election petitions."
Q. "Being yourself very conversant with election law?"
A. "Perhaps I have seen as much as any man living of election petitions. I do not ask advice very much on practical points."

When he died *The Times* remarked, "Probably our future electoral system will never create, nor need, a second James Coppock."

It is with the system which created and apparently needed James Coppock that Mr Gash is concerned. Its basis was the Reform Act of 1832, the principles and results of which Mr Gash subjects to an exhaustive analysis in his first four chapters. In retrospect it is abundantly clear that the changes made in 1832 ultimately produced, as their logical and inevitable result, the system of universal franchise which we know to-day. It is also clear that hardly a single member of the unreformed House of Commons would have voted for reform on such a scale, or perhaps for any reform at all, if he had appreciated the consequences of his action. The Tories did appreciate the consequences. "I was unwilling to open a door," Peel said, "which I saw no prospect of being able to close." "On this high historical and philosophical plane," Mr Gash observes, "the Tory case against reform was irrefutable." But, as he goes on to point out, there was one overwhelming argument against the existing system: the country at large was no longer inclined to put up with it. It might, in theory, be the best system in the world, but in the view of the mass of opinion in nearly every class it did not work. "What the Tories said was true; but what the Whigs did was necessary." . . .

The politics of the years which followed could be expressed, without absurdity, in terms of a personal relationship; of a marriage, for instance. There had been an emotional crisis, nearly resulting in separation or divorce. It was something not to be much talked of, certainly something not to be deliberately repeated but, rather, to be averted by all sorts of accommodations, arrangements, shifts, evasions. Occasionally, in moments of exasperation, one party or the óther might regret that the outright, deadly clash of principles had been prevented; in moments of pessimism its eventual coming might be prophesied; but for most of the time the terms of accommodation were accepted, at first consciously as the alternative to worse things and later as a matter of habit.

These terms involved the factors which Mr Gash writes of: bribery, corruption, undue influence, violence. It is not a pretty story and the characters in it, from James Coppock downwards, are not knights errant. It is quite enough to disabuse anyone who may still hold it of the belief that after 1832, as by a miracle, electoral purity replaced electoral corruption. There is some evidence, indeed, that in the first election after the Reform Acts corruption was at its minimum; not merely because electoral agents had not yet suited their arrangements to the new state of things but because the new electors were conscious of the trust imposed in them and anxious to discharge it honestly. Neither of these conditions lasted; many of the new electors proved as amenable to bribes as the old; and the technique of corruption no doubt benefited from improving habits of business and ease of communication as much as the ordinary commercial enterprise did. Mr Gash's sixth and seventh chapters, on "Electoral Violence" and "Corrupt Boroughs," make salutary reading.[2] . . .

[2] The student of public morality will be obliged to make a number of fine distinctions when he examines the attitude of mid-Victorian voters towards bribes. In some constituencies he will find the continuance of an old practice of paying a small sum, perhaps five or ten shillings,

Then there is the suggestion that the upper classes deliberately used their superior wealth and social power to corrupt the poorer voters and so to extend the term of their political supremacy. The difficulty here, which Mr. Gash illustrates by more than one example, is that refusal to bribe, in a habitually corrupt constituency, almost invariably meant loss of the election. It is impossible to say which of the two parties, the bribers and the bribed, took the initiative in establishing a system of bribery; but once such a system had been established there existed a section of the electorate which demanded bribes, or at least extensive treating, as the price of voting. Whatever else can be said, it cannot be said that money was forced upon an innocent and virtuous lower or lower-middle class by an upper-class bent on political debauchery. Most of the candidates would have been delighted if they had not had to spend a penny but their constituents often offered them no choice.

It would be very much of a mistake to suppose that these aspects of Mr Gash's subject offer nothing more than illustrations of the axiom that politics are a dirty game. They offer a great deal

to each voter who would accept it. Quite often the same amount was paid by each party, and in such cases it really corresponds to the efforts made nowadays by appeals in the Press and through loudspeaker vans to get people to vote at all. In another class of cases, not much dissimilar, voters accepted payments in money to vote for the party for which they would have voted in any event. It is obviously impossible to say how much was effected by bribery in the most reprehensible sense of the term—that is, the payment of money to induce a voter to vote in opposition to his previously held convictions. There are instances of voters deliberately organizing themselves for bargaining purposes. In the Barnstaple election of 1852, for instance, a number of new voters formed such an association and appointed a secretary to treat with the rival candidates.

more than this. For one thing, they throw light on the movement after 1832 for parliamentary reform in the sense of the further extension of the franchise. It was a well-known fact that the poorest voters were those most susceptible to bribes. This naturally led to the argument that the effect of further enfranchisement, by increasing the proportion of this class of voters, would only lead to an increase in corruption. This was one of the arguments which Robert Lowe used against parliamentary reform in the later 'sixties and it was not immediately easy to controvert it. Then, again, it is difficult to believe that some of the unenfranchized who demanded the vote were not, in fact, demanding a political privilege which they knew (from the experience of their more fortunate neighbours) was capable of being turned into ready money. This is at least as reasonable an assumption as that the vote was invariably demanded for altruistic or even for class reasons. The Maldon family who, by means of rigid organization and judicious bargaining, netted seventy or eighty pounds on the occasion of each election must have been regarded with envy, if not with admiration, by a good many of their acquaintances.

Ours is not a notably law-abiding age but in our attitude towards elections we are most notably law-abiding. We approach them with an austerity which we do not normally practice in other spheres of life. Indeed, it is as though we performed the act of voting in an atmosphere saturated with some kind of moral antiseptic. A hundred or a hundred and twenty years ago this was not the case. Politics were very much more closely related to ordinary life and ordinary habits than they are now. They were not insulated from violence and corruption; they were at least as violent as life in general and more corrupt. It would perhaps be paradoxical to argue that this was a good thing; but there is a case to be stated for it. The electorate was still very small. Was it better that the voters should be wrapped up in some sort of moral cotton-wool or that they should be exposed to the forces and influences which did, in fact, dominate society? This brings us to the chief, or at least the best, argument against voting by secret ballot. When the voters were few in number it was essential for the peace of the country and for general acceptance of the parliamentary system that they should be seen to cast their votes with the maximum of publicity. The possession of a vote was a privilege, even a privilege which could be turned into cash. But it could only be turned into cash if it was used, and the use of it demanded on occasion considerable courage: it might easily involve running to the polling-booth under a shower of stones and having one's clothes torn off on the return journey. . . .

Equally important considerations arise from other aspects of Mr Gash's book. In several vital ways the political system and the political morality of the day hindered the development of the party system. Since contested elections, even "pure" elections, were expensive affairs it was quite impossible for any one organization to attempt to call the tune throughout the country by paying the piper. Neither the Carlton Club nor the Reform Club had vast funds at its disposal for purposes of elections; money was difficult to collect and only too easy to disburse. On very special occasions a sum of £500 or so might be advanced towards the expenses of a candidate who was thought particularly worth supporting and who declined to stand without such a subsidy, but £500, in most constituencies, was small change. Conversely, a man who had perhaps spent £1,500 on winning a seat and another £500 on defending it against an election petition, was not likely to regard himself as the bondslave of the party whips.

Then, again, the very violence and turbulence of contested elections made reasonable and peace-loving men averse from them. Even if one party was likely to win both seats in a two-member borough it might be as well to avoid a contest by letting the other party have one. Or, at a later stage, when election petitions had been set down for hearing, such men as Coppock and his professional opponents on the Conservative side were accustomed to set off one against another, as insurance companies do with small claims under "knock-for-knock" agreements. Such compromises were legally and officially frowned upon; they were apt to infuriate petitioning candidates who found their claims summarily disposed of behind the scenes; but they took place, as all but the most innocent knew; and, as Mr Gash shrewdly points out, they did ensure rather more representation to the weaker party than it would have gained on a purely arithmetical basis if every seat had been contested at the polls and before a parliamentary committee. Though proportional representation did not exist, something of the effect of proportional representation was achieved by the combined forces of local prejudices, corruption and more or less corrupt compromises. Hence, parties were very far from being the strong and compact organizations we know and governments, in this period, were often weak. . . .

Mr Gash would not claim for a moment that he has written a political history of this period or has dealt at length with its political theories and aspirations after 1832. We have had, in fact, a good many descriptions of those theories and aspirations; sometimes, one thinks, too many. It is a salutary relief to be told how a specific technique worked. We have been tempted too often to regard England in the years which Mr Gash writes of as a land of flat misery in which wage-slaves dragged out a laborious existence at the behests of the Gradgrinds and Bounderbys. It is as well that we should see examples of the life that was lived at the same time: corrupt, exuberant and, as the psychologists might say, emotionally satisfactory.

Bibliography

Nineteenth-century British history has yet to find its bibliographer. Ironically, although the historical literature of the period is vast, there is no comprehensive and systematic guide to it, such as, for instance, those available for the three earlier centuries of English history. However, the interested reader can orient himself by consulting several works. He should begin with the relevant sections of George Matthew Dutcher *et al.*, *A Guide to Historical Literature* (New York, 1931) and its companion, George Frederick Howe *et al.*, *The American Historical Association's Guide to Historical Literature* (New York, 1961). He will also find an annual listing of books and articles on British history in A. Taylor Milne's *Writings on British History, 1934–39* (London, 1937–1953) and his two-volume compilation under the same title for 1940–1945 (London, 1960). To supplement Milne, see Louis B. Frewer, *Bibliography of Historical Writings Published in Great Britain and Empire, 1940–1945* (Oxford, 1947); Joan C. Lancaster, *Bibliography of Works Issued in the United Kingdom, 1946–56* (London, 1957); and William Kellaway, *Bibliography . . ., 1957–60* (London, 1962). The *Annual Bulletin of Historical Literature* also provides a useful listing. The footnotes and bibliographies of several of the works included in this pamphlet contain extensive references that should be consulted. Annotated bibliographies that can serve as guides to the period also appear in E. L. Woodward, *Age of Reform, 1815–1870* (London, 1962); A. Aspinall and E. Anthony Smith (eds.), *English Historical Documents*, vol. 11, 1783–1832 (London, 1959); and S. G. Checkland, *The Rise of Industrial Society in England, 1815–1885* (London, 1964).

For a firsthand view of the development of the controversy over reform, see "Parliament," Part II of Aspinall and Smith's *English Historical Documents*. This section also includes abridged texts of the English, Scottish, and Irish reform acts. The discussion in Parliament can be followed in *Hansard's Parliamentary Debates*, 3d series, and pro-reform reporting of day to day events can be found in *The Times* (London). A Tory review of the events of each year of the period is given in the *Annual Register*.

For general histories of the period, the following volumes, from which selections have been taken, are standard: G. M. Trevelyan, *British History in the Nineteenth Century and After* (London, 1937); J. A. R. Marriott, *England Since Waterloo* (London, 1913); Élie Halévy, *History of the English People in the Nineteenth Century*, 6 vols. (London, 1949–1952); and Asa Briggs, *The Age of Improvement* (London, 1959). The most detailed account will be found in the Halévy volumes for the period 1815–1852. For a thorough discussion of politics and social conditions from a nineteenth-century Radical point of view, see Spencer Walpole, *History of England from the Conclusion of the Great War in 1815*, 6 vols. (London, 1890). George C. Brodrick's *Political History of England from Addington's Administration to the Close of William IV's Reign (1801–1837)* (London, 1906) sees the reform as a completion of the work of the seventeenth-century revolutions and concentrates more fully on Parliamentary politics. Woodward's *Age of Reform*, cited above, is a cautious and balanced treatment of the period but accepts the concession theory of reform. H. W. V. Temperley devotes about half of the chapter

"Great Britain (1815–32)" in the *Cambridge Modern History,* vol. 10 (New York, 1911), to the reform controversy, and J. A. Hawgood in "Liberalism and Constitutional Developments" in the *New Cambridge Modern History,* vol. 10 (Cambridge, 1960) treats the Reform Bill in about two pages, comparing it with Continental developments.

One should not pass general accounts of the period without considering the works of three contemporaries. Harriet Martineau devotes the first four chapters of the second volume of her *History of England during the Thirty Years' Peace (1816–1846)* (London, 1849–50) to a strongly Whig version of the events which is valuable as a source for that viewpoint. John A. Roebuck and William Nassau Molesworth were active Radical supporters of the Reform Bill and their accounts reflect their participation. Joseph Hamburger used Roebuck's *History of the Whig Ministry of 1830* (London, 1852) and Molesworth's *History of England from the Year 1830–1874,* 3 vols. (London, 1871–1873) extensively for his study of James Mill and the reform.

The state of the pre-reform Parliament is detailed in Edward and A. G. Porritt, *The Unreformed House of Commons,* 2 vols. (Cambridge, 1909), and Joseph Grego, *A History of Parliamentary Elections and Electioneering from the Stuarts to Queen Victoria* (London, 1892) illustrates pre-reform election techniques in colorful detail. Betty Kemp traces the changing relationship between the House of Commons and the Crown in *King and Commons, 1660–1832* (London, 1957), as does A. S. Foord in "The Waning of 'The Influence of the Crown,'" *English Historical Review,* LXII (1947), 484–507. A. S. Turberville examines *The House of Lords in the Age of Reform, 1784–1837* (London, 1958) and concludes with an essay on "The House of Lords and the Advent of Democracy, 1837–67." A. Aspinall sketches some of the characteristics of parties in "English Party Organization in the Early 19th Century," *English Historical Review,* XLI (1926), 389–411.

The origins of the Parliamentary reform movement lay far back in the mid-eighteenth century. An older work, G. S. Veitch's *The Genesis of Parliamentary Reform* (London, 1913), traces Radical activity from 1768 to its suppression during the French revolutionary period and has a final chapter summarizing the reform movement to 1832. The first three volumes of S. Maccoby's *English Radicalism* (London, 1935–1955) cover the same period in much greater detail. W. L. Mathieson in *England in Transition, 1789–1832* (London, 1920) discusses various humanitarian and political reform movements from a liberal point of view, and Philip Anthony Brown, *The French Revolution in English History* (London, 1918) includes a final chapter on the overtones of the French revolutionary spirit up through the Reform Act. C. B. Roylance Kent in *The English Radicals* (London, 1898) traces Radicalism from John Wilkes to his own time, largely in terms of the personalities of the leaders. Élie Halévy's *Growth of Philosophical Radicalism* (London, 1928) is a classic study of the ideas of the Benthamite Radicals. Henry Jephson in *The Platform: Its Rise and Progress,* 2 vols. (London, 1892) discusses the use of a political platform as a rallying point for reform from the time of Wilkes and devotes the early part of the second volume to the Reform Bill agitation. E. P. Thompson's *The Making of the English Working Class,* Parts I and III, deals with the changing Radicalism of the working class from 1790 to 1832; Thompson suggests a stronger revolutionary strain than do most authors. From the Tory point of view, K. G. Feiling in the later chapters of *The Second Tory Party, 1714–1832* (London, 1951) describes the reactions of the Tory party to the Radical assault.

E. P. Thompson, in the book just cited (chaps. 11 and 12), also supports the view of Methodism as a conservative, antirevolutionary force that helped accommodate the working classes to the rigors of industrialization. J. L. and Barbara Hammond in "The Defences of the Poor," chap. 13 in *The Town Labourer* (London, 1917), take the same position. On the other hand, Maldwyn

Edwards in *John Wesley and the Eighteenth Century* (London, 1933) discounts the relevance of Methodism to England's avoidance of revolution at the end of the eighteenth century. E. J. Hobsbawm goes further in "Methodism and the Threat of Revolution in Britain," *History Today*, VII (1957), 115–124, reprinted in his *Labouring Men* (London, 1965), and in "The Labour Sects," chap. 8 of *Primitive Rebels* (Manchester, 1959), to suggest that some varieties of Methodism and Radical reform were found together. Although concerned with a slightly later period, F. C. Mather's *Public Order in the Age of the Chartists* (Manchester, 1959) is a helpful study of governmental machinery to keep order in the face of threatened violence.

The published papers, memoirs, and biographies of leading political figures are one of the richest sources for nineteenth-century British history. A number of the leaders who participated in the reform struggle or their intimates have left materials that give firsthand insight into the period. Lord Grey's son, Henry, the third Earl Grey, edited his father's correspondence with the king in *The Reform Act: the Correspondence of the late Earl Grey with His Majesty King William IV . . . from November 1830 to June 1832*, 2 vols. (London, 1867). Another son, Rollo Russell, offers the papers of one of the authors of the Reform Bill in *The Early Correspondence of Lord John Russell, 1805–1840*, 2 vols. (London, 1913). Lord Brougham, Lord Chancellor in Grey's government, provides his own account of the reform in the third volume of his *Life and Times of Henry, Lord Brougham*, 3 vols. (New York, 1871). However, his version must be used with care and the reader may find it helpful to consult A. Aspinall, "Lord Brougham's 'Life and Times,'" *English Historical Review*, LIX (1944), 87–112 for some cautionary warning on the use of this account as a source.

Several lesser figures who were close to government leaders also supply important information in their papers. Dorothea, Princess Lieven, knew the major political figures well, and L. G. Robinson's edition of *The Letters of Dorothea, Princess Lieven, during her Residence in London, 1812–34* (London, 1902) and Guy Le Strange's *Correspondence of Princess Lieven and Earl Grey* (London, 1890) are valuable for personalities and politics. Charles Greville was clerk to the Privy Council from 1821 to 1859 and not only learned a great deal about politics but also gained the confidence of successive political leaders. The first two volumes of *The Greville Memoirs*, most recently edited by Lytton Strachey and Roger Fulford, 8 vols. (London, 1938) provide an informed commentary on the reform period. *The Creevey Papers*, edited by Sir Herbert Maxwell, 2 vols. (London, 1904) present amusing party gossip from Thomas Creevey, a Whig member of Parliament and treasurer of Ordnance in the Grey government from 1832 to 1834. A. Aspinall, *Three Early Nineteenth Century Diaries* (London, 1952) offers selections from three political diarists of the reform period and includes a lengthy introduction on the politics of the period.

On the Tory side, the Duke of Wellington's views are available in A. R. Wellesley, Duke of Wellington, *Despatches, Correspondence and Memoranda of the Duke of Wellington*, 3d series, 1819–1832, 8 vols. (London, 1867–1880). The second volume of C. S. Parker's *Sir Robert Peel from his Private Correspondence and Papers*, 3 vols. (London, 1891–1899) contains material on the reform struggle. The correspondence and diaries of John Wilson Croker, the Tory secretary of the admiralty and confidant of many of the leaders, are available in *The Croker Papers*, edited by L. J. Jennings, 3 vols. (London, 1884).

There are biographies for all of the major political figures of this period. Some of them are the standard massive Victorian "Life and Times," favorable to their subjects and reprinting long extracts of correspondence. Other are less bulky recent works that attempt a more balanced view of their subjects. G. M. Trevelyan's *Lord Grey and the Reform Bill* (London, 1920), while very sympathetic to Grey, is the best study of the prime minister. J. B. Atlay provides a short study of Lord Brougham in *The Victorian Chancellors*, 2 vols. (London, 1908) ; Frances Hawes' *Henry Brougham* (New York, 1958) offers a more recent treatment and Chester W. New's *Life of Henry Brougham* (Oxford, 1961) covers the years before 1830. For other government leaders, see Sir D. Le Marchant, *Memoirs of John Charles Viscount Althorp, Third Earl Spencer* (London, 1876) ; W. M. Torrens, *Memoirs of the Right Honourable William Second Viscount Melbourne* (London, 1878) ; Lord David Cecil, *Melbourne* (New York, 1954) ; Chester W. New, *Lord Durham* (Oxford, 1929) ; Leonard Cooper, *Radical Jack* (London, 1959) ; and Spencer Walpole, *Life of Lord John Russell* (London, 1889) . C. M. Wakefield's *Life of Thomas Attwood* (London, 1885) provides a biography of the leader of the Birmingham Political Union, and Jessie K. Buckley offers a study of *Joseph Parkes of Birmingham* (London, 1926) . For working-class Radical leaders, see G. D. H. Cole, *Life of William Cobbett* (London, 1924) ; Graham Wallas, *Life of Francis Place* (London, 1918) ; Samuel Bamford, *Passages in the Life of a Radical*, 2 vols. (London, 1844) ; and Alexander Somerville, *Autobiography of a Working Man* (London, 1951) . For Tory leadership, see Philip Guedalla, *Wellington* (London, 1931) and A. A. W. Ramsay, *Sir Robert Peel* (London, 1928) .

Some of the most interesting work on the Reform Bill is concerned with local history and adds to the variety shown in the Asa Briggs selection. Briggs himself has contributed several articles to the literature: "The Background of the Parliamentary Reform Movement in Three English Cities, 1830–32," *Cambridge Historical Journal*, X (1952) , 293–317; "Thomas Attwood and the Economic Background of the Birmingham Political Union," *Cambridge Historical Journal*, IX (1948) , 190–216; and "Social Structure and Politics in Birmingham and Lyons (1825–48) ," *British Journal of Sociology*, I (1950) , 67–80. See also volume I of Conrad Gill and Asa Briggs, *History of Birmingham*, 2 vols. (London, 1952) , which includes the reform period. Other studies of local areas are Norman Gash, "Brougham and the Yorkshire Election of 1830," *Proceedings of the Leeds Philosophical Society*, VIII (1956) ; G. P. Jones, "The Reform Movement in Sheffield," *Hunter .Archaeological Society*, IV; A. S. Turberville and F. Beckwith, "Leeds and Parliamentary Reform, 1820–1832," *The Thoresby Miscellany*, XLI; and A. T. Patterson, *Radical Leicester: a History of Leicester, 1780–1850* (Leicester, 1954) . L. J. Saunder's *Scottish Democracy, 1815–1840* (Edinburgh, 1950) provides a good social and intellectual background .to the reform movement in Scotland, and R. B. McDowell's *Public Opinion and Government Policy in Ireland, 1801–1846* (London, 1952) includes an account of Irish politics in the 1830s.

There are numerous assessments of the effects of the Reform Act after 1832. An older, although still very useful, study of the development and operation of the franchise is Charles Seymour's *Electoral Reform in England and Wales* (New Haven, Conn., 1915) . A more recent study of the terms of the Reform Act and the conduct of constituency politics is Norman Gash's *Politics in the Age of Peel* (London, 1953) , reviewed by W. L. Burn among the selections. A stimulating article by D. C. Moore, "Concession or Cure: The Sociological Premises of the First Reform Act," *The Historical Journal*, IX (1966) , 39–59, extends the ideas expressed in Moore's selection and suggests a very different interpretation of the Act's purpose. Sir Ivor Jennings' *Party Politics* 3 vols. (London, 1960–62) is helpful for the post-reform period. C. S. Emden in *The People and the Constitution* (London, 1956) discusses the development of the concept of popular mandate in Parliament from 1832. S. F. Woolley examines "The Personnel of the Parliament of 1833" in the *English Historical Review*, LIII (1938) , 240–262, and J. A. Thomas does the same for a longer period in *The House of Commons, 1832–1901* (Cardiff, 1937) . A. V. Dicey's classic series of *Lectures on the Relation between Law and Opinion in England* (London,

WESTMAR COLLEGE LIBRARY

1914) sees 1832 as a milestone in the development of Benthamite liberalism. Walter Lyon Blease in *A Short History of English Liberalism* (New York, 1913) offers a brief discussion of the Reform Act followed by a chapter on "Middle Class Supremacy." R. B. McCallum, *The Liberal Party from Earl Grey to Asquith* (London, 1963) and Donald Southgate, *The Passing of the Whigs, 1832–1886* (London, 1962) trace important developments in the Liberal party. George S. R. Kitson Clark in *Peel and the Conservative Party* (London, 1929) credits Peel with the rehabilitation of the Conservative party after 1832. Norman Gash in "Peel and the Party System, 1830–50," *Transactions, Royal Historical Society,* 5th series, I (1951), 47–69, takes a more limited view of Peel's contribution. H. W. C. Davis's Ford Lectures of 1926, published posthumously as *The Age of Grey and Peel* (Oxford, 1929), review the character of the Whig and Tory parties between the 1760s and 1852.